Joe Stahlkuppe

Great Danes

Everything About Selection,
Care, Nutrition, Behavior,
and Training

BARRON'S

²CONTENTS

UNDERSTANDING THE GREAT DANE

To understand the physical aspects of the Great Dane, one must combine the height of the Irish Wolfhound, the presence of the Mastiff, and the athleticism and sweet disposition of the Greyhound. To emotionally understand the Great Dane, one must imagine an overly large young boy possessing the most tender of hearts.

Meet the Great Dane

It may seem unnecessary to introduce one of the most recognizable dog breeds in the world, but the Great Dane that many people think they know may not be the real Great Dane at all! Dane breeders and owners point out that their calf-sized pets attract a lot of attention when out in public—on walks, at dog shows, and at dog parks. People who wouldn't think twice about commenting on a Doberman or a German Shepherd Dog will often approach Dane people with some questions about the dog, her size, how much she eats, and so on. The Great Dane is a real attention-getter.

Sensitivity: What many casual observers do not know is that the huge, perhaps even awe-inspiring, big dog has many attributes that make her a unique pet. For example, under the big, tough exterior, Great Danes are often quite sensitive. Some owners report that an unintentionally loud reprimand can cause a Dane to withdraw to a safe area in the home for perhaps a lengthy period of time.

Danes often physically lean against their beloved humans, and Daisy Dane (our female Great Dane representative) did this with a beloved but wobbly toddler, causing the young child to fall down. The toddler, who was also learning to talk at about the same time, pulled herself up by grabbing firmly onto the Dane's muzzle, looked the dog straight in the eye, and proceeded in unintelligible baby jabber to berate the careless canine. The child's parents found the deeply chastened Dane in her crate looking

The Size Factor

Throughout this book there will be a recurring theme—"Giant dogs bring giant responsibilities!" It is crucial that any Great Dane owner or prospective Dane owner understand this. Although ownership of a Great Dane can be immensely pleasurable, ownership of a dog of any giant breed also requires extra thought, planning, and care. The normal situations and circumstances confronting every dog owner are magnified when the dog stands 3 feet (1 m) high at the shoulder and weighs as much or more than the owner.

very sad indeed. It was some minutes before the dog would come near the child, who had already forgotten the incident.

Malleability: Another Dane trait that may not be widely known is their high degree of malle-

ability and resilience. A Great Dane can become spoiled, aggressive, or even too passive when humans allow them to become so. Great Danes have done well in obedience work, the show ring, Schutzhund work, and as pets. A cruel owner who habitually mistreats a Dane could get a giant, dangerous dog for his efforts. A lazy owner who will not take control and help a Great Dane become a good pet may get a stubborn dog that tries to dominate her humans. An owner who has obtained a good-quality Great Dane from a reputable source and has planned, prepared, and cared for her can realistically expect to get a super super-sized pet.

Physical Appearance: From a physical standpoint, the Great Dane is almost a contradiction in terms—elegant/strong, artistic/powerful. Not only is the Great Dane great in height, it is also muscular without the heaviness of the Mastiff, Saint Bernard, or Newfoundland, but with more substance to go with its tallness than the Greyhound or Scottish Deerhound. The Dane has the regal bearing and demeanor that has often been presented in sculpture and paintings.

Great Danes have six currently American Kennel Club (AKC) accepted colors: black, blue, brindle, fawn, harlequin (a predominantly white dog with jagged black spots of varying sizes), and mantle (formerly referred to as "Boston" because of the black with a white collar look similar to that of the Boston Terrier). Too much white on the chest of a black, blue, brindle, or fawn Dane is strongly frowned upon. Unaccepted colors include blue merle, which are like harlequins with a blue base color; fawnequins, which are white dogs with large ragged fawn or brindle spots; and white Danes (often blind or deaf).

History of the Breed

We do not know precisely when this giant breed originated. We do know that dogs resembling Great Danes have been in the company of humans for hundreds of years. While some British breed authorities do not agree, the Great Dane appears to be largely a German creation, and one in which Germany takes considerable pride. It is also true that a very similar dog to the Great Dane was evolving in England and that modern Danes probably do owe some debt to these early British dogs, in addition to the German contributions to the breed.

The ancestors of the Great Dane were most likely of hunting stock. Since the Dane is a taller, trimmer counterpart to the English Mastiff, it is probably related to the Mastiff in some way. The Dane has even been called the "German Mastiff" in several countries.

German Popularity

Many well-known Germans owned Great Danes. Notably, Otto von Bismarck loved Great Danes and did much to further the breed. One of the most fabled Germans of all time, Manfred Von Richthofen, the Red Baron of World War I aviation, owned a Great Dane named Moritz and would often put the big dog in the second seat of his plane and take the Dane up into the world of early manned flight.

Great Danes, in whatever country, were originally hunting dogs, especially for the fearsome and dangerous European wild boars. These boars bore little resemblance to barnyard porkers and were tough and potentially deadly.

Hunting boars required a dog of courage, speed, and exceptional power. The early Danes fit this model and succeeded admirably at the task.

The large boarhounds made a logical transition from a purely hunting dog to a protective guard dog. This change took place over many years and required added attributes other than just the ability to hunt boars. Protection dogs had to be more people-oriented, of less violent temperament, and able to do tasks other than hunt boars.

The onetime boarhound first became a guard dog and then a family pet. Almost from their beginning as a recognized breed, the Great Dane was embraced by the dog breeders and citizens of Germany—so much so that the Germans came to admire the Great Dane and it became the "Deutsche Dogge," or the German Mastiff.

The Germans put stringent requirements for the breeding, care, and training of the "Deutsche Dogge." By setting tough rules and adhering to them, the Dane was not only a large elegant dog, but also a large, powerful, and useful dog.

The Great Dane Standard

Each recognized breed in the AKC has a written standard or blueprint that should be referred to and followed by all licensed dog show judges, reputable breeders, and current and potential dog owners. This standard acts as a clear guide to how a perfect specimen (size, disqualifications, shape, color, temperament, and so forth) of that breed should look and act. Since a 100-percent perfect dog (in any breed) is probably impossible to achieve, the breed standard sets a high goal of excellence for judges, breeders, and owners to aspire to reach. The national

What's in a Name?

One fact is clear: the Great Dane is in no way Danish! For some reason now lost in the mists of the past, the French naturalist Buffon referred to this breed as the "Grande Danois," or "big Danish," and this name, though still not used in Europe, was grasped by the English-speaking world.

Ironically, one of the most identifiable breeds in the world still has different names in different places. The Great Dane of England, the United States, Australia, and New Zealand is the "Alano" in Italy and the "Deutsche Dogge" in Germany. While the names are different, the various breed standards remain very similar (all patterned on the German version). The Great Dane then is no Dane at all, but the German national dog that is claimed by the British and misnamed by a Frenchman. Even with all this name confusion, the Great Dane remains one of the most unique and popular giant dogs.

breed clubs constantly monitor what they have set in their breed standards. When conditions or circumstances call for a review and potential modification of the standard, the breed clubs carefully (and often over months or years of study and debate) make necessary changes.

The Great Dane Club of America (GDCA), established in 1889, has been the major authority for the Great Dane's development, registration, promotion, and overall support for more than 123 years. The GDCA has produced, over the past many decades, the standards by which the Great Dane has been judged and acknowledged. Many other nations, like Canada, the United Kingdom, and Germany have similar standards in use in their respective countries.

Any serious newcomer interested in Great Danes should consult with the GDCA and the AKC about the Great Dane standard. Wise newbies will spend much time studying, discussing with experienced Dane breeders, and visualizing the dog in the verbiage of the standard with real Great Danes at dog shows and other locations. Contact the AKC or GDCA (by phone, regular mail, or via e-mail), and you can obtain a Great Dane standard of your own. (*www.akc.org* or *www.gdca.org*)

The Great Ear Controversy

To crop or not to crop might seem to be the question for the future for some Great Dane enthusiasts. The ear trimming that sometimes is done on Great Danes is called cropping, and there are strong voices both for and against it.

Originally, when the Great Dane was the boarhound, its ears were cropped to protect them from the tusks of the large wild boars. Later, the aristocratic look of the cropped ears was kept more as an attractive feature than as a hunting precaution.

Ear cropping is still often used on show-quality Great Danes in the United States but is not practiced in many other countries. The AKC standard for the breed does not oppose the practice, and gradually, uncropped Danes have become more accepted in breed competition. As of right now, the decision as to whether your Dane's ears should be cropped is left up to you.

If you are going to have ear trimming done, cropping should be done at about seven weeks of age by a skilled veterinarian, experienced with Great Dane cropping, who feels comfortable with the practice. After their ears are cropped, Dane puppies must be securely bandaged to hold them in place and to keep the youngsters from pawing at their still-tender ears.

The Nature of the Breed

It is certainly true that the Great Dane possesses impressive size, but size alone is not what makes the Great Dane great. The regal bearing, the expressive face, and the dignity of the dog make him memorable, along with his grand proportions.

To understand the Great Dane, one must acknowledge that the aggressive nature of the boarhound/guard dog had to be modified into a more placid, yet still watchful, demeanor. As the early Great Dane breeders solidified the breed type, they were ever vigilant in trying to produce a giant alert dog who would always be safe around people and other animals.

Although a sensitive nature is definitely a part of many Great Danes, it would be an error to brand these huge dogs as giant softies or mammoth pushovers. A well-trained Great Dane from a good genetic background, in a home setting where the humans involved are knowledgeable and well prepared, can be an awesome pet. Great Danes usually greatly want to love and be loved in return by their humans. The Danes that do best are those who spend the most time with their families.

Great Danes as Family Pets

For the family that wants a really big canine member, and that is willing to take responsibility for a bigger than big dog, the Great Dane can be a superb addition. For the single person with adequate time to give a Great Dane the care and training he will need, the Dane is also an exceptional choice.

Great Danes exiled to the kennel or to the backyard for days or weeks on end become kennel and yard dogs whose personalities may not advance much past a big dog out back who eats, sleeps, poops, barks, then starts this sad perpetual cycle all over again. To sentence any dog, espe-

cially a Great Dane, to such a life is ignorant, uncaring, and definitely a form of animal abuse.

Knowing their place in the family hierarchy, Great Danes can become great family members, and can fit into most of the family activities. While a large home with a large, high-fenced yard would be the best situation for any giant dog, Great Danes given adequate training and sufficient exercise have shared condos and apartments with their owners. The degree to which a family or individual has a successful outcome owning a Great Dane is directly proportional to the level of commitment that family or individual is willing to give.

Great Danes in Obedience

Great Danes are not seen in obedience trials with the same frequency that one sees German Shepherd Dogs, Golden Retrievers, and some other breeds. A number of Danes have, how-ever, done very well in their pursuit of obedience titles.

Obedience trials, licensed by the American Kennel Club (AKC) offer the following titles (which go after the dog's name, as in Tartaro's Thunder Thud of Long Island, C.D., or Barr's Daisy Dane of Hauppauge, C.D.X.) for the dogs and owners who are willing to put in the training time to learn an increasingly difficult group of tasks: Companion Dog (C.D.); Companion Dog Excellent (C.D.X.); and Utility Dog (U.D.) Guidelines on what is required and how to get involved in obedience trials are available from the AKC (see Information, page 92).

While most dogs can certainly be improved with appropriate training, for a dog the size of a Great Dane, training is essential. In obedience work, as in regular training, the dog must be under the control of a human being and not the other way around. Obedience training

The Blue Merle?

As was once the case with the now-accepted mantle Great Dane color pattern, an unaccepted color—blue merle—has been a by-product of harlequin breeding for many years. Blue merles are similar to the harlequin in that they both have ragged black patches as a part of their color pattern.

Where the merle differs from the harlequin is that the merle's base color is blue or bluish, while the harlequin's base color is pure white. Merles cannot be shown in Dane classes in AKC shows and may be good pets, but they are not considered to be rare or exotic.

a Great Dane can be a very rewarding experience, but also possibly a frustrating one. Not every dog, including every Great Dane (or every Great Dane owner), is a good candidate for the discipline and hard work required to be successful in obedience work.

Great Danes as Show Dogs

One famous breeder/exhibitor of harlequin Great Danes once suggested, "Perhaps one reason that this breed does so well in the show ring may be because Great Danes are always on exhibition in one form or another." Danes do seem to attract a lot of attention, even when they are just out for a walk with their owners. Even at dog shows where Great Danes are often seen, a really excellent specimen will attract the attention of viewers who would never classify themselves as Great Dane enthusiasts or perhaps not even Dane fans! Perhaps it is the combination of size, structure, demeanor, power, and elegance that captivates onlookers.

Great Danes as Guard Dogs

The Great Dane is an impressive guard if he just stands still and barks. It is as a deterrent that the Great Dane does his best work as a guard dog. Certainly, some do reasonably well in guard dog training. As a breed, Danes just don't seem to relish such work like Dobermans, Rottweillers, and some other breeds do. That Danes are not as often seen in the Schutzhund competitions where trained dogs attack well-padded "enemies" is probably viewed as a real positive by the people who wear the padded suits. Great Danes may not relish guard and attack work like some breeds, but when motivated to attack, a Great Dane is an awesome, intimidating force.

If you want a live-in pet that will give his life to protect you, a Great Dane is a good choice. If you want Thunder Thud (our male Great Dane representative) to be an all-out attack dog solely for the purpose of serving as a 24/7 guard, do yourself and him a favor—choose another breed!

LIVING WITH A GREAT DANE

One Great Dane owner likened living with the breed as "driving the Budweiser Clydesdales (and their beer wagon) through crowded city streets at rush hour, or a National Basketball Association seven-foot-tall basketball star trying to be comfortable living in a child's playhouse." Size is the predominant factor in sharing your life with a Great Dane and simply can't and won't be ignored.

"Great" Means Bigger than Big

As an adult, Daisy Dane is much larger than a German Shepherd Dog, a Collie, or even a Rottweiler—all breeds appropriately thought of as "big" dogs. At maturity, most Great Danes will be able to easily put their chins on the surface of the average dining room or kitchen table.

The length of the average Dane's body when full-grown will exceed, even before the tail is included, the height of most adult human males. Such a long body requires sufficient turning and maneuvering space in a home, kennel, run, or yard. The weight of the average adult Great Dane will be as much as most teenagers and many adult humans. A large Great Dane can actually occupy much more space on a couch (if she is allowed to be on a couch) than two average-sized humans.

Daisy Dane's tail is a mighty whip that can, in one swish, sweep a coffee table clean of China cups or bric-a-brac. Her tail can knock a toddler down with her enthusiastic wagging. A Great Dane that jumps up on people (a very bad habit to allow any dog to learn) can topple larger children and smaller adults. The toenails of an excitable Dane puppy can rake furrows across furniture, flooring, or human skin.

Add to the physical aspects of Dane ownership the fact that these dogs are fond of leaning on people and things, whether the people or things are capable of withstanding such demonstrative affection. Older people and children need to realize that Danes like to physically be next to the people they love; therefore, they should brace themselves for the leaning onslaught of an adoring dog.

Although these physical aspects would seem to point to making Daisy Dane a purely outside pet, that should not be the case. Great Danes certainly enjoy some time outside every day; they like taking walks or spending time in a yard or a kennel run, but they also adore their humans and will want to spend time with them inside.

Great Danes and Children

Great Danes can be excellent companions for children. Some Danes seem to have an innate love for these little humans, and other than the accidental falls that a big dog can cause a small child, the two get along well together.

Children are sometimes less reliable than Great Danes in being gentle and kind. After they get over their initial awe at such a huge dog, some children cannot be trusted not to injure

even this biggest of dogs. Children must be reminded that this is a dog and not a pony or inanimate object and that the dog is not to be ridden, kicked, or struck. Very small children or even not-too-trustworthy older children should always be supervised by an adult when they are allowed to spend time with a Great Dane.

While Great Danes are normally very good with children, responsible parents should always teach their children that a strange dog is not to be approached until an adult says it is okay to do so. Parents should also instruct their children that there are times when any dog, even a Great Dane, may not be in the mood to be a good playmate. When a dog is eating, when a female has puppies nearby, or when the dog is injured are all times when the dog is best left alone. Overly aggressive dogs should never be allowed to be near children, and overly aggressive children should never be allowed near dogs.

Great Danes with Other Dogs

Great Danes are not usually bullies. They don't usually have to be. Their size alone seems to intimidate all but the feistiest dogs. While male Danes are like many males in many breeds—territorial as far as other male dogs are concerned—unless a strange dog is actually intruding into a Dane's space, he won't have too much to fear from the big dogs.

Generally, a Great Dane can easily adapt to life with other dogs in the household with no more difficulty than most other breeds. Of course, bringing two strange adult unneutered males into the same household and expecting them to act like playful puppies shows little awareness of dogs and their behavior.

Ironically, Dave Nasser of Tucson, Arizona—the owner of the 43-inch (190-cm) tall Giant George currently listed by Guinness World Records (2011) as the "Tallest Dog in the World" and the "Tallest Dog Ever"—concedes that this giant of giants is often afraid of small dogs like Chihuahuas.

Great Danes with Other Pets

Many Great Dane breeders relate how their Danes not only get along with cats and other family pets, but actually come to be great pals with other animals in the home. As with strange dogs and the Great Dane, a good dose of preparation laced with common sense is appropriate here. If you bring an adult Great Dane that has never been around small animals into a home setting, there may be some problems. If a Dane puppy is raised with other pets, she comes to view them as part of the home, and generally no problems ensue.

Great Danes and Strangers

Great Danes are not always fond of strangers. These dogs like to know what they will encounter in their environments. A visitor in the home who is accepted by the Dane's owners may be treated with a cool reserve at first. After a person has shown that he or she is no threat to the home or her owner, Daisy Dane may dole out a variety of responses, ranging from benign disinterest to lavish adoration.

Great Danes that have been thoroughly socialized as youngsters will have no trouble accepting mannerly strangers either in or outside the home. The very size of the Dane alone is enough to discourage strangers from causing difficulty for such a dog's owner. Danes can be the gentlest of dogs, but they are still dogs; they don't always understand that a child, another animal, or a stranger doesn't mean them (or their humans) any harm. Part of the responsibility of being a Dane owner is anticipating, desensitizing, or eliminating situations that Daisy Dane might see as hostile or threatening.

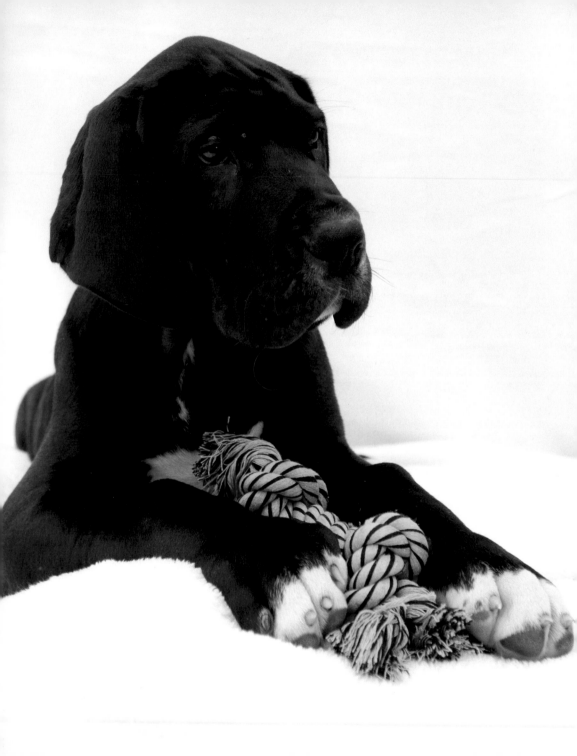

CARING FOR YOUR GREAT DANE

While a Dane does take up a great deal of space within a home, it is within this home that he can come closest to reaching his true potential as a companion animal. Caring for such a dog begins and ends with the amount of time, awareness, and effort you are willing to expend.

Housing a Giant Dog

The fact that the space needs for Great Danes are different than for Schnauzers, Corgis, or even Afghan hounds is understandable and even obvious. Just what those space needs are may not be as clearly understood. It has been suggested that a prospective Dane owner take a yardstick or a measuring tape around the house and measure potential problem areas so that an adult Great Dane can be kept out of troublesome situations as much as possible. Great Dane height is but one concern; its weight and the length of its body even when on all fours must also be taken into consideration.

The Crate

The best method of allowing a dog to live inside is to provide for him, from his very first night in your home, a cage, crate, or carrier that will be Thunder Thud's own special place within the household (see Crate Training, page 49). In the wild, canines will be born in and spend a good portion of their lives in and around a lair or den that is thought to represent a place of safety from the outside world.

By using this denning behavior of dogs, humans have been able not only to make dogs, like the Great Dane, feel safer and more comfortable within a home, but also to use this behavior as an aid in training (see Housetraining, page 48).

The Yard

The outside area around Thunder Thud's home also deserves some consideration. Giant dogs demand giant responsibility in this area, too. A backyard or kennel fence that could keep many smaller breeds securely inside is

nothing more than an easy jump for a Great Dane. Most Dane breeders believe that a fence should be at least 6 feet (1.8 m) high to keep a giant, athletic dog inside it.

The construction of the fence is also important. Danes are, as mentioned, "leaners." If a 150-pound (68-kg) dog leans on a poorly constructed fence, door, or gate long enough, it may fall. Also, some Danes are great diggers and can somehow squeeze their big bodies *under* some fences that they can't go over.

Exercise

Great Danes, although very big and athletic dogs, are somewhat calmer than some other breeds. Certainly a Dane that lives inside needs adequate exercise to keep him healthy. Great Danes must have daily exercise to keep them in good physical and mental shape. This type of exercise can come in the form of regular walks with their owners or other members of their families. Thunder Thud and you will benefit from being out in a park or on safe walking areas, being together for a special time on a consistent basis, and being able to both get all the cardiovascular benefits that come from steady strolling.

Because a Dane weighs 150 pounds (68 kg) and the human can weigh less than that, control of the dog must rely on more than sheer physical domination. An out-of-control Chihuahua can be scooped up into the arms of his owner and thus can be kept from a harmful situation. Not many people will be able to handle a Great Dane in the same way. Always be prepared to avoid potential problems when you are out on a walk with a Dane, and try to avoid becoming overly complacent, which could tend to allow Thunder Thud to get into a bad spot. Proper training will ensure that your walk with your Dane is both safe and beneficial.

Grooming

Grooming a Great Dane is a good deal easier than grooming many other breeds. Because there is so much more of a Great Dane, simplified grooming is no small blessing. Keeping the big dog clean and presentable should be no huge task, but there are some points that need to be handled:

✔ Because the Dane's face is so much a part of the beauty of the animal, make every effort to keep the Dane's ears, eyes, muzzle, and chin clean. These are also areas that are difficult for your dog to clean himself.

✔ Weekly brushing with a stiff bristled brush should keep Thunder Thud's coat in great shape.

✔ Don't bathe Thunder Thud too often. Too-frequent shampooing will make his coat and skin dry and possibly flaky. If he gets really dirty, then a bath is (of course) necessary.

✔ Pay close attention to cleaning your Dane's teeth. This is a grooming task best started when Thunder Thud is still a puppy.

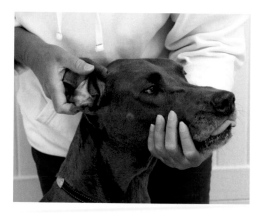

✔ Feet and toenails need regular inspection. It is very important to keep a Great Dane's nails evenly trimmed (another task best initiated in puppyhood) to avoid any foot problems, which can be aggravated by the large size and weight of the adult Dane (see Toenails, page 88).

✔ Keep watch on toenails and footpads during your regular inspections for external parasites. Fleas, ticks, and ear mites can make Thunder Thud (and you) miserable and could possibly spread diseases.

Boarding Your Great Dane

Boarding your Great Dane is a very plausible alternative to the rigors and stresses of extended travel with your dog. There are several options for boarding your Dane:

✔ There are many quality boarding kennels across the country that are accredited with the American Boarding Kennel Association (ABKA) (see Information, page 92). The ABKA teaches its member kennels in the best ways to care for their clients' pets. Some boarding kennel owners will possess the coveted, "Certified Kennel Operator"

(CKO) designation showing that they have skillfully applied their craft and have passed numerous tests.

✔ Thunder Thud may be able to stay at home under the care of family, friends, or neighbors.

✔ Enabling your dog to stay in his own home with a professional pet sitter (who always should have references and be insured) who will take care of your dog is another option.

✔ Your Great Dane's veterinarian may have some extra space for your dog at his or her clinic.

✔ Under certain circumstances, if Thunder Thud's breeder lives nearby, maybe this person won't mind having a visiting alumnus stay for a few days.

CONSIDERATIONS BEFORE OBTAINING A GREAT DANE

Self-examination is important before you and your family invite any pet into your home to share the pluses and minuses of your home life. Such a fearless personal investigation is all the more crucial when that pet is a dog, and when that dog is a Great Dane.

Illusion and Reality

There are many things about the breed that can make a Great Dane a truly special pet in the right home. There are also some aspects of Dane ownership that may be incompatible with your household. Deciding if this breed fits your needs, wishes, and expectations is a task that no Great Dane breeder, dog authority, or book can do for you. This decision must be made by you and the other members of your family. Failure to seriously undertake this task may result in some inconvenience for the humans involved, with almost inevitably tragic results for the dog.

It is sad to say, but Daisy Dane as an actual dog often suffers from an inability to live up to the vision of an unrealistic fantasy dog. Some people buy a Great Dane in order to have the biggest, meanest dog in their neighborhood. Others have a mental picture of strolling in the park with a magnificent Dane drawing the admiration and envy of passersby. Still, others envision themselves lounging in their book-lined den with a giant canine companion stretched out at their feet.

These fantasies are easy to imagine. Making these dreams a reality is quite another matter. The person who wants Daisy Dane in order to have "the toughest dog in town" definitely needs rethinking and perhaps long-term therapy. The Great Dane can certainly fill the size part of this fantasy, and some Danes could conceivably become vicious enough to satisfy any maladapted dog owner, but such behavior runs counter to her genetic makeup and is absolute cruelty to the animal.

A Great Dane owner can surely look forward to sharing peaceful moments within a home setting. Daisy Dane does have a reasonably low activity level and can be an excellent home companion, but not without adequate preparation and training. Developing her into an acceptable member of a household requires caring, knowledgeable, consistent help from the humans in that household. This task will not be accomplished in a split second, like the mental vision version, but will take adequate time and sufficient effort.

Remember that, first and foremost, a good Great Dane should be a good pet. She should be compatible with you and your family, with your family circumstances, and with the realistic things you want a pet dog to be or do. One of the most rewarding aspects of dog ownership is to take a young, impressionable pup and shape her into a truly excellent adult dog.

Searching for the Right Dog

Having decided that you and a Great Dane are right for each other, you now have to find just the right Great Dane for you. This process will take some time and effort on your part. While Great Danes are not rare, the dog or puppy that has the just right temperament, health history, potential, color, sex, age, and so forth may not be easy to locate.

Where to Look

If you have studied the breed at dog shows, you may already know some Great Dane owners in your area. This is an excellent place to begin

your quest. Talk with several of these Dane experts, ask questions, and take notes. Find out their recommendations on where to seek the dog you want.

Sources: There may be a Great Dane breeders' organization in your city or state. There may also be a Great Dane rescue and adoption group in your area. After you have presented yourself as a serious and well-prepared potential Dane owner, most of these breeder or rescue groups should be willing to help you locate the dog you are seeking. In fact, these organizations may be the only way you can find exactly what you want. Great Dane experts generally will know who among their peers has a litter of pups, perhaps an older pet-quality puppy, or even an adult Dane in need of a good home. Because these are the people that really care about Danes, this is probably the only way to go about finding a potential show dog, a healthy pet, or a Great Dane in need of the love you have to share.

If you have trouble finding a local Great Dane club, contact the national club (see page 92) or the American Kennel Club (AKC) (see page 92) or a Great Dane rescue and adoption group for information. The AKC also has an excellent DVD about Great Danes. An investment in this DVD would probably be a very good idea for any potential Dane owner.

There are magazines and websites available that specialize in Great Danes; some of these are listed on page 92. By learning as much as you can about as many Dane sources as you can, you will be

━━ T I P ━━

Beware of Puppy Mills

Many breeds and types of dogs are quite popular. Popular breeds (like the Great Dane) often have opportunism, greed, and dishonesty as fellow travelers. Newspaper classified ads, bulletin boards, Internet sites, and other public forums will often include advertisements about Great Danes. While some of these ads may be from innocent parties trying to sell Dane (or half-Dane) puppies to good homes, many others aren't so innocent. Puppy mills are a curse on purebred and mixed-breed dog ownership.

These greedy, cruel, and perpetual puppy retailers care little or nothing about the mothers that whelp these pups, the pups themselves, or you. Your money is ALL they have any regard for. Be sure that you are acquiring your Great Dane from a reliable source.

in a much better position to choose the place from which to obtain your Dane.

You may also find a great deal of information on the Internet. Whether you visit shows, contact breeders or adoption groups, or read magazines or books, always remember that you are looking for the Dane that best fits your family. Don't accept anything other than a wonderful Great Dane.

In your search for a Great Dane, you must clarify your objectives. Just what do you want this dog to do for you? If you are seeking a show dog, go to dog shows. Talk with the top breeders of Great Danes today and discover if they have the show prospect you're seeking. These people may also know of pet-quality puppies available for your inspection.

Breeders

What Should Be Expected of You

Great Dane breeders will be more than willing to help an aware newcomer find a good dog or puppy, but they are serious about their dogs and will generally expect some things from you. They may want evidence that you are serious about wanting to own a Great Dane and want to give Daisy Dane or Thunder Thud the best of all possible homes. They may also want to know about your experience with

other dogs. Will this Dane be your first dog? You may want to take good care of a Great Dane, but do you really know how?

Some breeders (and rescue groups as well) will question your reasons for wanting a Great Dane. Be prepared and not offended by this quizzing. Recognize that the vast majority of Dane people only want to make certain that a puppy or an adult dog doesn't end up in abusive, neglectful, or ignorant hands.

What You Should Expect

When you approach a Great Dane breeder about a puppy or an older dog, you should expect honest answers from a knowledgeable source. Try to find a breeder whose good reputation is as important as the producing of good Great Danes.

You should generally expect to pay several hundred dollars (or more) for a healthy, pet-quality dog, and perhaps several thousand for a top show prospect Great Dane. Beware of bargains. The dog-owning world is full of people who, to save some money, took a lesser quality puppy than they really wanted. Some Dane buyers choose to buy their pups from sources other than reputable breeders and soon discover that the bargain puppy becomes the most expensive pet they have ever owned.

In a breed where the potential for health problems is admittedly higher than in some others, you *must* seek out the healthiest Great Dane possible. Your Great Dane is not only a financial investment, he is also a canine friend who will share your home and life for hopefully a decade or more. Can you afford to buy a close-companion animal without having as much documentation and information about him as possible?

Papers

Prior to actually selecting a puppy from any source, make certain that the Dane you may buy has these vital documents and necessary records.

Health Records

Current health records showing all vaccinations with dates, wormings with dates, and examinations by a licensed veterinarian, including the results and treatments.

Pedigree

An accurate pedigree showing the puppy's parentage and family tree. The Great Dane Club of America has some strong recommendations about what colors of Danes should be mated together. Be sure that your potential pup's pedigree shows that these color-breeding recommendations have been followed. This pedigree should also show the champions or obedience title holders in your prospective pup's ancestry.

AKC Registration

The AKC registration certificate confirms that this Great Dane puppy is purebred, with his mother (dam) and father (sire) both being AKC registered Great Danes. You should also receive application forms to forward to the AKC in order to register this puppy, if you do buy him, in your name.

CHD Screening

You will want documented evidence that the parents of this puppy are free from Canine Hip

Dysplasia (CHD) (see Hip Dysplasia, page 77). While this does not ensure that their offspring will not become dysplastic, the tests—which are performed after a dog is two years old—are the best screening techniques currently available.

If you can't get this paperwork, you should not buy the puppy. Don't accept the puppy on the proviso that "the papers are in the mail." Most Dane breeders are honest, but a puppy should be viewed as a very important purchase and it is your responsibility to make sure good business practices are followed.

Most of all, you should expect that your study and careful search for a Great Dane who you will share your life with will result in a healthy, temperamentally sound puppy without any genetic defects or inherited physical problems. Your entire experience as a novice Great Dane owner will certainly be affected by your ability to be a knowledgeable, assertive, and careful consumer.

Guarantees—From Both Sides

Most responsible Great Dane breeders will give you a written health and temperament guarantee for any puppy they sell. This guarantee should be in writing and should specify that the dog's inherited health and temperament is guaranteed for the life of the animal. Quality breeders should be confident of the quality (health and otherwise) of their dogs.

Reputable breeders (as well as rescue/adoption organizations and animal shelters) will usually have some requirements for you, too. Since many Great Dane breeders take the dogs they sell as a lifelong responsibility, they may have some agreements for you to sign.

Spaying or Neutering

One such agreement involves your commitment to have spayed or neutered a pet-quality dog or puppy, in order to prevent an inferior specimen from producing inferior puppies. This does not imply that the dog or puppy has any physical or temperamental shortcomings; it could mean that its color may not be just right or that some other minor cosmetic flaw is evident. Some breeders make a practice of withholding the registration papers until the dog or puppy buyer brings proof from a veterinarian that the animal has been spayed or neutered.

Adoption organizations and shelters fully realize that there are far too many puppies of all types (including Danes) being born each year. Almost certainly, as a Great Dane newcomer, you will not want to add to this glut of puppies that will need homes in an environment where homes are far outnumbered by puppies.

If you take your time in choosing an adult Great Dane, you may find just the perfect dog for you and your family. You may be able to help retrain or readapt a maladjusted adult. Many adult Great Danes are desperately in need of a good family to whom they may belong. Through no fault of their own, these full-grown dogs have lost their human pack, and their lives will be sad and incomplete unless they can find a new one.

Puppies require a lot of time and effort to become the kind of pet you are seeking. A novice dog owner should probably choose a puppy and let the youngster grow up with the family as the family learns how to train and care for their pet. As adaptable as some older Danes can be, a puppy is learning the lessons he is taught usually for the very first time. No re-training or restructuring is required with a youngster that will know only what you taught him.

Returning the Puppy

Many Great Dane breeders (and adoption agencies and shelters) will want to be certain you understand that they maintain a strong original ownership interest in the Dane you are buying. If you cannot keep the dog or puppy, the breeder will probably want you to agree to return the pet rather than pass him on to someone else.

A Puppy or an Older Dog?

The choice here is largely determined by what you want in a Great Dane. If you have had considerable success as a dog owner and merely want a loving companion, there may be an adult Great Dane, perhaps from a rescue group or shelter, that could move right in and become your best friend forever. Some adults and older puppies just don't work out with their initial buyers. In other cases, circumstances may necessitate the return of the Dane to the breeder. Quite often these Great Danes can readily adapt to your home and lifestyle. Other dogs, however, have picked up bad habits or made attachments to their former owners that may be hard to break.

A Male or Female?

Your expectations for your Dane will also influence your decision about the gender of your pet. Male Great Danes are larger than females, and they possess a masculine bearing and presence that one sees in most males. Intact (non-neutered) males will be more territorial than females, and perhaps more likely to attempt to escape from the backyard in order to "cruise" the neighborhood.

Although they tower over males and females of most other breeds, female Great Danes should be decidedly feminine in their graceful and elegant appearance. They are somewhat less aloof with strangers and other dogs than are males. Unspayed females go into heat with the estrous cycle about every six months and have to be safeguarded during this time to prevent unwanted litters, so owning a female has its own set of concerns.

A properly trained, well-bred Great Dane of either sex should be an excellent pet for the right family. If you don't have any serious aspirations as a Great Dane breeder, then either sex—with the male being neutered or the female being spayed—should prove right for you.

Pet Quality or Show Quality?

A pet-quality Great Dane is not less healthy, less temperamentally sound, or—other than

cosmetically—less of a Great Dane than a show-quality dog. A show-quality Dane should also not sacrifice health or temperament in order to be a show dog. Both categories of Great Dane should be able to become excellent companion animals.

Because truly great show dogs are rare in any breed, a puppy with show potential is significantly more expensive than a puppy already identified as a pet prospect. Furthermore, as a newcomer to Great Danes and in the show ring, you have little chance of being allowed to own a really top-flight show puppy unless you agree to provide the puppy every possible chance to achieve her show ring potential.

Choosing a Great Dane Puppy

By this time you and your family have decided if you want a Great Dane puppy. You have given the matter considerable thought and study. You have assessed your household's capacity to provide a good home for a Great Dane. You have visited a number of sources and have seen what really good Great Danes look like. You have talked with, and perhaps even visited with, some Dane breeders and adoption sources and have seen their dogs and their homes. You have puppy-proofed your home and had a high fence erected around the backyard. You now seem ready to choose a puppy.

Several sources (breeders or adoption/foster groups) near your home have litters of Dane pups in colors that you like. You have decided that a healthy, pet-quality female puppy with a good disposition is just what you want. You

recognize that there is enough demand, even for pet pups, that the price or fee may be several hundred dollars.

Take time to observe the puppies; watch how they interact with each other and with their mother. Carefully handle each puppy, paying attention to the ones who seem alert, unafraid, and well adjusted. After you have carefully looked at each pup, ask the breeder or foster home about the puppy that you like best.

Commit to buying Daisy Dane only after *your* veterinarian has examined her and found her to be healthy and free from serious defects, including obvious temperament issues. Then, and only then, have you found your new canine family member.

BRINGING HOME YOUR GREAT DANE PUPPY

The first in-home contacts with you and your Great Dane are crucial to the future of your relationship. Carefully choreograph these first contacts and your early moments with your new Dane. Bad habits (both canine and human) begun early often take longer to undo.

The Initial Phases

Getting to know Thunder Thud while he is still at the breeder or foster setting is usually a good idea. If a few brief visits and playtime with him, without his dam or siblings present, are possible, he will be leaving his first home with friends instead of strangers. Even this brief introduction to you can certainly aid your puppy. This bonding period may not be necessary or possible with every pup, but if the opportunity to ease yourself and your family into young Thunder Thud's life presents itself, by all means take it.

The Trip Home

The use of a crate/cage/carrier for your travel with your Dane is always recommended when transporting a canine by car. Be sure to bring a couple of old towels to put in the car-rier (or in case the pup suffers from motion sickness).

If your initial trip home with Thunder Thud is a long one (several hours or more), be sure to plan rest and relief breaks at least once each hour. Even though he is still a relatively small puppy, you *must* be sure that you have a collar and leash on him anytime he is out on these breaks. A puppy can get into harm's way before most humans can react. Prevention, in the form of a good collar and leash and an alert attitude, could save Thunder Thud's life even before he gets to his new home.

Early Training

When you arrive, even before you take the puppy inside, take him *immediately* to a pre-selected urination and defecation spot. You may want to "salt the mine" by dropping some litter from the puppy's first home, which has his urine and/or feces scent. This will encourage the pup in learning that this site is where such activities are to be done. Remember that this first relief time is very important; stay with Thunder Thud in this location until he relieves himself, and then enthusiastically praise him for doing the right thing, at the right place, at the right time.

Puppy-proofing Measures

You most certainly should have puppy-proofed all the areas to which the youngster will have access. Puppy-proofing means that you have removed from these places everything that could harm an innocent, ignorant,

and inquisitive puppy. Some of these things are:

- Tight squeezes—behind a stove or upright piano or between banister railings, where a puppy could get trapped or caught.
- Heavy items on tables that could tip over or fall on a puppy.
- Stairwells, patios, porches, or open windows that could lead to a possible fatal fall.
- Access to common household items (household cleaners, air fresheners, poisonous houseplants, antifreeze, exposed wiring, or extension cords) that could kill your puppy if ingested or chewed.
- Small, easy-to-swallow things that could harm Thunder Thud, such as tacks, pins, rubber erasers, and children's toys.
- Doors and gates to the outside that a quick Dane puppy could dart through or get caught behind and injured.

Thunder Thud will grow rapidly. The tabletop that was secure from a curious Dane puppy two months ago may be right within reach now. Do a complete puppy-proofing job the first time, and update your efforts every week or so as the young giant matures.

Adjustment Time

When your puppy first comes to your home—his new home—there should be an adjustment time when the puppy is given the affection, care, and early lessons that will help him quickly fit into the household.

A responsible person, probably an adult or older teenager, should have enough time with Thunder Thud to help him understand some of what is happening in his young life. Much of what he encounters now will be mystifying and

bewildering. Until the recent memories of his old family—his mother and littermates—begin to fade, this young Great Dane needs loving support from his new family.

It is natural to want to show Thunder Thud off to anyone and everyone, but give him a little time to get to know you and the other members of your household before you spring a whole group of new people on him. Many things are new for him, and the more interruption from the regular pattern of his new life, the longer it will take for Thunder Thud to adjust.

Helping Your Puppy Settle In

Thunder Thud may be just a young puppy, but he is at his learning peak. The lessons he is

taught now and the impressions he gets now can stay with him for the rest of his life. It is your role as human leader and puppy owner to see that he gets the right lessons and the right impressions. In the absence of your guidance, Thunder Thud may reach the wrong conclusions about what he is supposed to do and what he is allowed to do.

The trip home inside a noisy machine with strangers may have been certainly puzzling and perhaps even frightening to an eight- or nine-week-old Dane puppy. Hopefully you have already begun to teach him the right place, outside, to urinate and defecate. Whoever is in charge of Thunder Thud's adjustment period should try to get the puppy outside to the relief place on as timely a basis as possible. Certainly, no noses should be rubbed in

Simple Aids to Ease the Early Days (and Nights) of Adjustment

There are some things that you can do to help make Thunder Thud's settling in ordeal easier.

- Using one or two plastic 2-liter soft drink bottles (with tops securely tightened) filled with hot to warm water and wrapped in an old beach towel will give the pup a sense of warmth somewhat like his mother.
- Perhaps something from the pup's first home that has retained comforting scents could be placed in the carrier to provide him with a little "home" scent.
- Some people use an old wind-up alarm clock (non-electric, with the alarm deactivated for sure) so that its ticking somewhat simulates the beating of his mother's heart.

- One of the more unusual ways to comfort a puppy is to place a radio near (not in) the carrier and turn it on low volume on an all-night talk radio station, which gives the puppy some sense of not being alone.

Foods

Other aids in helping Thunder Thud settle in involve feeding the same food he has been eating before he came to you (see Feeding Your Great Dane, page 61). Changing foods at this crucial time can only add to the physical trauma of his move to a new home. It is also a good idea to feed the puppy on the same schedule he was on at the breeder's or foster home. Regulating when the puppy eats is also a good way to project when he will need to go to his relief place outside.

Exercise

Don't let your new Great Dane puppy over-exert himself. Playing with Thunder Thud is fine, but he is still a very young puppy and should only play in very short spurts. When the puppy appears to be tiring, take him to his carrier for a little rest. This tends to reinforce the idea of just what his den is for—a place for rest and sleep.

Remember that Thunder Thud is only a Great Dane puppy. Don't expect anything but puppy behavior out of him. These initial days are for first lessons, adjustment, and settling in. If you take things slow with the pup now, you'll have a stable foundation on which to build the other training that will come in a few months.

urine and no physical punishment should be meted out to an ignorant pup for making a mess. (see Housetraining, page 48). If given the right training in a consistent fashion, most Great Dane puppies can quickly understand where they can and can't go. (With no lessons or the wrong approach, some dogs may NEVER learn.)

By using the crate as a resting place for the puppy and as a regular place for him to stay when he is not with you, Thunder Thud already has a safe and comfortable base to run to if he gets tired of playing or if he feels unsure or afraid. Your puppy will now have to adjust to being alone without his mother or littermates. In some ways, his new family can replace the old, but this should NOT happen with regard to sleeping arrangements. It may be cute to let a young puppy sleep with you, but how cute will that be with a 150-pound (68-kg) adult Great Dane? Let Thunder Thud sleep in his carrier. You'll be happier and so will he!

Now is a time when the entire family must pull together and do what is best for the baby Thunder Thud. Beginning with the first night in his new home, no matter how much pitiful puppy wailing or how much human hand-wringing there may be, Thunder Thud sleeps in his carrier, *period*. Everyone in the household needs to know that this is best for the puppy, and although it may appear to upset him, it is really much better for the Dane in the long run.

When he is placed in the carrier for the first night Thunder Thud will naturally be lonely, a little frightened, and anxious to have his new humans come and comfort him. *Don't do it, and don't allow anyone else in the family to do it!* No matter how much you paid for this

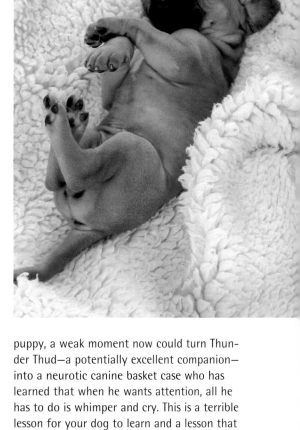

puppy, a weak moment now could turn Thunder Thud—a potentially excellent companion—into a neurotic canine basket case who has learned that when he wants attention, all he has to do is whimper and cry. This is a terrible lesson for your dog to learn and a lesson that may be very hard to unlearn!

Steel your resolve and that of your family with the knowledge that your puppy, if left alone, will not continue to cry much beyond the first few days. Consistency now will be a great aid in helping this Dane puppy reach his potential as a wonderful family companion.

THE ADOPTION OPTION

Being placed in an animal shelter or in an adoption organization is a shock and is bewildering to any dog. Daisy Dane, through no fault of her own, has been uprooted from the safety and sanctity of her pack family. Such a life-jarring experience may happen to many thousands of pet animals each year— some of them like Daisy Dane, whose life is in a state of flux until some other pack family steps up to make her complete once again.

Adult Great Dane Availability

A surprising truth about the dog pounds and animal shelters in the United States is that as many as 25 percent of the dogs in need of a new life are purebreds! Some of these are Great Danes. Some potential pet seekers visiting these shelters are intimidated by the size of the adult Great Dane, so many Danes sadly go unadopted from shelters and municipal dog pounds.

Some of these giant dogs have become homeless through no fault of their own. An owner's death, a divorce, or a change in living arrangements are some of the reasons given for giving up an adult Great Dane. Sadly, some potential pet owners were overwhelmed by the rapid growth and large size that their cute Dane puppy morphed into. Ill-prepared owners are certainly a part of the reason for the number of adoptable adult Great Danes. Other sources for adult Danes are animal cruelty raids made on puppy mills and animal hoarders. Through it all there are, in every part of the United States and Canada, significant numbers of adult Danes waiting for new homes, new humans to love, and new lives.

Adoption Locations

There are several national organizations and numerous regional, state, and local Great Dane adoption groups. Great Dane Rescue, Inc., is one source that can help you find the best possible adoptable adult Great Dane. This nonprofit organization has relationships and links to many places where adult Great Danes have been rescued from negative situations and have been fostered in caring homes until appropriate, permanent homes are found for these needy pets.

Adult Adoption Advantages

Great Danes, though sensitive and loyal to their original homes, are resilient and responsive to the care and love of their new homes. No Great Dane is too old to respond to a kind word or a tender touch in a new setting. There are many success stories about Danes coming from horrendous situations and finding love and bonding in adoptive homes. Regardless of the reasons that the dogs were surrendered from their initial settings, Great Danes are the *adaptable adoptables.*

Older Great Danes are often preferred over Dane puppies:

1. Adult Great Danes, especially those from Dane foster homes, have been housetrained and have much greater bladder and bowel control than the youngsters do.
2. Much of the personality of the adult dog has been formed and molded by the positive people in the adoption settings. Adult Danes can be aligned with new homes according to the need for a placid dog, a more athletic dog, or a dog that is good with other pets.
3. Older Great Danes have been through the "chewies" stage of puppyhood, where any immovable object is eligible to be gnawed, chewed, and clawed by a rambunctious Dane puppy.

4. Crate training is usually already complete for the grown-up Great Dane. Night whining is a thing of the past.
5. While Great Dane puppies are adorable, much of their lives are still in the future. A Dane adult's life, like most adult humans, is in the present. With such a dog, you know what you have and can immediately adjust without the surprise factor that exists with puppies.

Because of the wide and wonderful network of adoption organizations and their foster-care homes, many adoption-ready Great Danes already have had some obedience training.

- Minor health issues for adult Danes have already come to the surface and either have been dealt with or have become part of a treatment plan that goes with the dog to his new home.
- You can expect that adoptable Great Danes coming from these foster homes are vastly better pets than dogs obtained through a "free to a good home" ad in a newspaper or by word-of-mouth from an acquaintance or neighbor. Fostered Danes have been examined by a veterinarian before being made available for adoption to the public.

Administrative Aspects

Don't expect to drop by an adoption center and pick up a Great Dane on the way home from work like a loaf of bread. Finding the adult Dane a good and caring new home is the prime focus; if you can make the grade to be the Dane's new owner, so much the better.

Much like the careful questioning that reputable Great Dane breeders put prospective puppy buyers through, adoption facilities are

extremely thorough in assessing your likelihood to adopt one of their Danes. Simply put, these organizations want to avoid going through this process all over again if you and a homeless Great Dane fail to work out. The atmosphere seems to be that this Dane has "been there, done that, not anxious to do it again!"

Achieving an Adoption Attitude

The breakup of a Great Dane with his human pack can be upsetting, mildly annoying, or inconvenient to the humans involved. For the ousted Great Dane, this action literally turns his world upside down. The human beings that he loved so dearly and would have readily given his life for have abruptly disappeared. He is left with no pack, no best friend, and possibly no life expectancy. This adult Dane's life has now become a crapshoot, and only if the dice fall his way will there be much of a chance for any more happy times in his life.

This is unabashedly a plea to the readers of this book. Please consider an adult Great Dane as your next pet. If the idea appeals to you and you make the grade established by the adoption organizations, you could make all the difference in the world for a Great Dane in search of a family of his own.

TRAINING YOUR GREAT DANE

There is nothing more disconcerting in dog ownership than a dog that will not obey. Just seeing a Great Dane hurtling at top speed toward a dangerous or potentially disastrous situation, oblivious to the plaintive calls and quasi-commands of his owner, is both extremely frightening and absolutely unnecessary.

An Untrained Dane

It is foolish to own an untrained dog of any breed, but the height of folly is to possess a dog that you could not possibly physically restrain in any of a number of emergency situations. The Great Dane that will weigh as much or more than his owner must be under the control of a human in every possible circumstance. Some control measures include high fences, sturdy kennels, and strong leashes attached to strong collars, but the best control of all is adequate training

Thunder Thud may be a wonderful companion, a genuine member of your family, and a real canine friend and protector, but the best Dane in the world is still just a dog. Dogs will usually react to situations in dog-like ways. A bitch in season in the neighborhood can turn the calmest Great Dane into a hormonally super-charged Romeo. If Thunder Thud will not obey your call to come to you at an ambivalent and stressful time like this, he is not fully or safely trained and could present a danger to himself or others.

Training your Great Dane gives you an opportunity to build into the dog some restraints, some ingrained habits, and some specific behavior that you can control. Without this control you have a giant problem animal that could easily get into serious trouble. Protect yourself and protect your dog; *train him!*

Using Pack Behavior

Your Great Dane is a pack animal. In the days when the Dane went by the name Alaunt or boarhound, the breed was often kept in large packs for hunting purposes. Like these hunting packs, dog packs all have a leader and social hierarchy in which each individual animal knows exactly its own place. Puppies are taught pack behavior by their mothers and littermates before they ever leave the whelping box. Pack behavior is just as significant for your Great Dane as it is for any wolf living in the wild. By understanding pack behavior, you can use it to help you train Thunder Thud.

The "Alpha" Male Concept

Pack leadership always goes to the strongest animal. In dogs and wolves this leadership position is generally held by an adult male in his prime with sufficient life experiences to guide the pack in the business of day-to-day survival. Because size and strength play a key part in this concept, and male canines are usually larger and more powerful than their female counterparts, the leader of the pack is called the first or "alpha" male.

In the wild, the alpha male gets the best of the food, his choice of breeding-age females (usually known as the "alpha female"), and his will is law in the pack. The alpha male zealously protects his pack from other canines and will kill or banish any who challenge his authority. The alpha male remains the alpha male only as long as he is the smartest and strongest. When a stronger male comes along, the alpha male is usually deposed either by death or by running away from the pack.

You, your family, and your Great Dane make up a pack. You or some family member will have to assume alpha male responsibilities, and it is crucial that the hierarchy will have each human at a point above the Great Dane. You as alpha male will have to be stronger than the Dane. Installing yourself in this role usually comes much more easily when Thunder Thud is still a puppy. It is possible to become the boss of an adult Great Dane, but if that adult him-

self has been in the top spot, a stubborn clash of wills could result.

Because "nature abhors a vacuum," if you or some other person in your family fails to become alpha male, your Dane may try this position on for himself. When this happens, the proverbial cart is truly before the horse-sized dog. Unless you can reassert your leadership and move the dog down several notches in the "pecking order," you may have a difficult—if not potentially dangerous—situation. Imagine that you have a 150-pound (68-kg) canine tyrant in your home, one that will only do what he wants to do!

Failure by the human members of a household to take firm control has resulted in more than one potentially good Great Dane ending his life as an unwanted pet at the dog pound, or as a vicious dog chained to the bumper of a 1951 Studebaker in a junkyard. Don't let this unnecessary tragedy happen to your dog. As children need a clear understanding of the rules of the family and the lines of authority supporting those rules, so does your dog, whether that dog is a 10-pounder or whether he is ten times as large.

When to Begin Training

Some training has been initiated for you by your Dane's mother. She instilled in her puppies some early lessons while the pups were still unweaned babies. Her example as a dog trainer is a good one for you to follow in the additional training of her son or daughter. The training methods used by the mother Dane were:

- **Repetition:** Some behaviors were absolutely not to be tolerated, and behaving in this way brings instant correction.

=== T I P ===

What Dog Training Is All About

Getting your Great Dane to do what you want him to do is not cruel and isn't just some control game that you can use to show your friends and neighbors how you can manipulate a huge dog. Training your dog is as much for you and the members of your family as it is for the dog.

Before you can teach a dog anything, you have to decide what you want him to learn. You also have to decide on a "lesson plan" on how you will handle those things you wish to teach. By becoming even an amateur dog trainer, you will become a much better dog owner.

You will have to understand what your dog can learn before you can train him. By doing this you will have to become more acquainted with the learning needs of the dog.

If approached correctly and in the right frame of mind, training your dog will help him become a much better pet and companion and can very well be one of the most rewarding parts of pet ownership.

While you may go on to teach your Great Dane a wide variety of cute—even amazing—tricks, your first priority is to teach the dog things he needs to know to be a better functioning pet.

=== T I P ===

Bladder Control

No matter how much Thunder Thud may want to please you, until he is between four and six months of age he will have limited bladder control. Don't expect perfection until the pup matures physically enough to be able to wait to relieve himself. But this is certainly not intended to suggest that you wait six months to begin housebreaking. You need the mental lesson firmly in place when the pup's physical functioning reaches maturity.

- **Consistency:** Bad behavior was corrected the same way each time. The mother didn't punish a particular act one time and reward it or ignore it the next time, which can only confuse a puppy.
- **Timeliness**: Correction for bad behavior happened immediately, while the offending act could be associated with the resultant negative outcome in the young, impressionable puppy's mind.
- **Fairness:** The correction was fair and not overly severe. The mother dog will not normally do a puppy any real physical harm for a youthful indiscretion. A snarl or a rough nudge from their mother is all that most pups will need to get the general idea that they did something wrong.

As long as the puppies were under her control, these lessons were enforced. She didn't count on the pups remembering from one week to the next what was wrong the previous week. By repetition, consistency, and fairness, she taught her puppies their first lessons, which tend to stay with dogs for their entire lives.

If you follow this canine course in dog training, your job will be much easier, will fit itself into a pattern that most Danes already understand, and thus will have more of a binding effect on the behavior of the dog. Repetition, consistency, and fairness worked for the mother, and it will work for you!

Housetraining

Thunder Thud already started learning this important lesson on the first day you brought him home. When you immediately took the puppy to the specially designated spot for him to relieve himself and then enthusiastically petted and praised him when he did, you started housetraining your puppy. He needed to defecate or urinate and when he did so, at the place you chose, he was rewarded.

Housetraining a Great Dane puppy need not be the arduous activity that it has been made out to be. If your puppy does not make a mess inside, he will please you—and Thunder Thud certainly wants to please you. At this early part of your relationship, you and your puppy are in complete agreement. Now your part of the housetraining task is to help him continue to please you by not making a mess inside. The best way to do this is to understand some basic canine instinctual behavior and to use this behavior to help you help your puppy learn this lesson.

Crate Training

Crate training is the very best and easiest way to help your dog become housetrained. It takes advantage of a side effect of denning behavior. In the wild, animals rarely foul their dens or lairs; to do so would be self-defeating. Not only would a den be a messy, smelly place to live, but predators could more easily find it by following the smell of built-up urine and feces. It is for this reason that dogs, by nature, do not like to mess up their carrier/den (see Crate Training Suggestions, page 51).

Puppy Physiology

Some understanding on your part of puppy physiology is important. Knowing when your puppy will normally need to relieve himself allows you to establish a regular schedule of going outside. Here are some suggestions on how to time trips outside.

- Take the puppy out to relieve himself after he eats or drinks. The additional food or water in the pup's system causes additional pressure on the bladder and colon.
- Go outside the first thing each morning, *immediately after* the puppy is released from the crate.
- Go out after the puppy naps during the day.
- Go out after a long and lively play period.
- Go out as late at night as possible.
- Go out immediately if the puppy shows signs of wanting to defecate or urinate, like staying near the door, circling, sniffing, and looking generally uneasy.

Sometimes you will get the puppy outside just in time. When Thunder Thud relieves himself at the right place, elaborately praise him right away. Stay with the puppy until he does eliminate and until he has received his customary award of praise from you. This helps identify relieving himself with the sights and smells of this particular place and with the reward he can expect for doing the right thing. *Never*, for any reason, scold Thunder Thud at this special spot! This is where he expects to do his business and then be rewarded. If you scare or punish him at this place, he may become confused from the mixed message you are sending.

If he defecates or urinates inside, never hit him! A firm, alpha male–voiced "NO" will let Thunder Thud know that what he did was not good behavior. *Never* make matters worse by rubbing the puppy's nose in any urine or excrement. Such an illogical action will do absolutely nothing to help the pup learn, may possibly cause him to fear you, and will leave you with a messy puppy to clean up.

By feeding your Great Dane at regular times, you can usually anticipate when the puppy will need to visit outside. If you are using a highly digestible, premium puppy food, the pup's stools should be much firmer with much less volume. This aids colon retention and, if an

CHECKLIST

Crate Training Suggestions

- Have a positive attitude about cages/crates/carriers and the effective use of instinctual canine behavior in these, which serve as a den for your Great Dane.
- When you buy your first crate or carrier, buy it so it is large enough for the puppy to use as an adult, too. To keep the crate from being segmented by the puppy into a sleeping area and relief area (much like the paper training room), make a sturdy partition to keep the den no larger than the puppy requires, and then make the space bigger as the pup grows.
- Place the den in an out-of-the-way, but not isolated, place in the home. Be sure that the crate is not in a direct draft or in the sun, or the puppy will not be comfortable.
- Put the Dane puppy in the crate for rest periods or when you have to leave the dog unattended for a couple of hours. Upon your return, immediately take the pup out to the relief spot, praise his activity there, and come right back inside. If you want to

go out and play, do so *after* the break is over so the dog will not confuse elimination with exercise or play.
- Do NOT give enthusiastic praise or petting to the pup for about ten minutes after you let him out of the carrier to be with you in the home. Such praise may confuse the puppy and may make it seem that getting out of the carrier is to be rewarded.
- Use a stern, tough, alpha voice to quiet any crying or whining when the pup is placed back into his carrier.
- Keep a mat or old towel in the crate, along with a favorite toy or durable chew, to keep the puppy occupied when he isn't sleeping.
- Never feed or give water to Thunder Thud in his crate. The place for food and water is outside the crate-denning area.
- Your family and friends will need to understand the importance of the crate to your Dane pup's overall development. Don't let any member of the household upset the regimen that the puppy will become accustomed to after a few weeks..

error is made, the mess isn't as bad to clean up. In addition, *never* feed a puppy table scraps, even in small amounts. This habit can upset a puppy's system and the nutritional balance of a quality pet food. Feed the puppy about three

times a day, but don't leave food out continuously, as you will have no way to know exactly when the pup ate.

While crate training is certainly the best form of housebreaking, it may not work very well for people who can't help the pup get adjusted to the regular schedule of feeding combined with crate training. For those people who have to leave the puppy in a laundry room or a bathroom for the adjustment period, a second—perhaps not quite as effective—method for housetraining is available. This is called paper training.

Paper training involves the confining of a puppy to some easily cleaned room (a bathroom, kitchen, or laundry room). It does not work particularly well with outside training because the puppy is given two "right" places to go, but paper training may be necessary for those who cannot constantly stay with the puppy in his first few days in his new home. Paper training also works fairly well for people who live in apartments, where getting a puppy outside quickly may not be easily achieved.

Three basic areas are needed within this room when you are not with your puppy: a den

area (where the puppy's crate can be placed), a water and food area, and an elimination area. The elimination area should be covered with several layers of newspaper. The puppy will be encouraged to relieve himself in this specific place on the papers. If observed, the puppy should receive appropriate praise for going on the papers. Since most dogs don't like to soil their food and water area any more than they want to mess up their den, the elimination area needs to be some distance away from the eating and sleeping areas.

By using layers of newspaper, urine and excrement can be removed and disposed of by simply lifting the top couple of layers. The puppy's scent will remain, and this scent—just like it worked outside—will give the puppy an idea of what he is supposed to do here.

Paper training usually takes a little longer in housetraining a puppy. Even with paper training, be sure to walk the puppy early each morning and late each night, and also after meals when you can. Since your schedule prevents you from being with the puppy every time that nature calls, the paper training method is only a stopgap way of helping your puppy until he has matured more in bladder and colon control.

If your puppy has an accident somewhere he is not supposed to go, get that area cleaned up as soon as possible. Use an odor-neutralizing cleaner to get rid of the pup's scent. If a smell lingers, the puppy may logically assume that this, too, is an okay site to relieve himself.

If you live in an urban area and your puppy must be walked on city streets and sidewalks, *always* pick up and dispose of any excreta. Not only is this a responsible thing to do, it is usually the law!

Obedience Training

When to Start Training

A distinction is to be made between house-breaking; settling in and other early lessons that your Great Dane puppy must know; and the more formal training, which should not take place before the youngster is around six months old. Though some dogs are ready a little earlier or a little later, at this age Daisy Dane should be mature enough to actually gain something out of basic obedience training. You are the key in basic obedience training. You must be consistent, confident, and patient if the commands you want to teach are to be learned. Training is *not* a family function until all of the five basic commands (*sit, stay, heel, down,* and *come*) are thoroughly learned. One person must do the training, and the training, should be done the same way each time.

Training Equipment

In order to train your Dane, you will need a chain training collar (often mistakenly called a "choke chain"). This type of collar is both humane and effective when correctly and appropriately used. This chain collar, which is to be worn only during training sessions, does not choke the dog. The collar, when correct pressure is applied, causes the dog's head to come up with a slight snap. This is to get Daisy Dane's attention, and when applied with the stern "*no*," this combination not only controls and corrects, but the "*no*" lets her know that her action was not what she should have done.

The chain collar should be large enough to go over your Dane puppy's head at her widest part, with no more than 1 inch (2.5 cm) of

extra room. This collar must be removed after training and replaced with a regular collar that has identification and rabies vaccination tags attached. Leaving on the training collar not only fails to make use of Daisy Dane recognizing what is going to happen when this collar is put on her, but if an unattended dog should happen to snag such a collar on something, strangulation could occur when the frightened puppy tries to escape.

With the training collar you will need a 1-inch (2.5-cm) wide leash (sometimes called a lead) measuring 6-feet (1.8-m) long. This leash, which is *not* to be used on your regular walks with the dog, should be made of leather, nylon, or woven web, and it should have a sturdy, but comfortable, hand loop on one end. On the other end of the leash should be a securely attached swivel snap for attaching to the ring on the chain training collar.

Let Daisy Dane become thoroughly familiar with the chain training collar and the training leash. She must not fear these training aids if they are to effectively work. Let your puppy get the weight and feel of both on her neck several days before you actually plan to begin training.

The Five Key Commands

Before you begin to teach your pup, you need to teach yourself how to give commands effectively.

- Issue clear, one-word commands to your dog. Use the dog's name before each command, as in *"Daisy Dane, sit,* and be authoritarian in your tone—no place here for baby talk or endearments. You can play with her later, but right now you should be all about the business of training!
- Use the same tone of voice each time so that your pup will know by the intonation as well as by your words that you mean business.

- Don't confuse the dog by issuing several commands at one time, as in, *"Daisy Dane, come here and sit down."* Each command has a single, specific word, and that word should be used each time and in the same tone of voice.
- Remember the canine learning rules and use them:
  1. Praise enthusiastically.
  2. Correct fairly and immediately.
  3. Practice consistent repetition.
  4. Never, ever lose your temper.
  5. Be patient.

Patience

This last canine learning rule deserves some additional clarification. Don't try to take your pup out for a training session when you are angry or upset about something else. Daisy Dane will be able to hear the underlying hostility in your voice and may think that she is to be punished. Training works on a correction/ praise system, with no place for punitive measures. Wait until you are as less emotionally charged before you go out to work with the Dane puppy.

Keep lessons short (no more than twenty minutes). Stick to one new command at a time. Your pup will be doing well to learn all these commands over a period of months. Don't try to build Rome in a day. When the training session is over, don't immediately begin playing and roughhousing with your Great Dane; let twenty minutes go by to separate training time with the human with the authoritarian voice from playtime with the friend.

Note: Other members of the household need to understand that training a puppy is serious business. They also need to understand the basics of what you are doing with the pup, so that they will not inadvertently undo your training when they play with the dog.

Sit

Sit is a good command on which to start your Great Dane, as she already knows how to sit down. Now all you need to do is teach her when and where to do so. With the training collar attached to the training leash, place Daisy Dane on your left side next to your left leg, while holding the leash in your right hand. In one continuous, gentle motion, pull the pup's head up as you push her hindquarters down with your left hand, giving the firm command "*Sit*" as you do.

When she is in the sitting position, lavishly praise her. Using the concept of continuous repetition, repeat this lesson until the puppy sits down without having her rear end pushed downward. Remember to keep the same upward pull on the leash to keep the *sit* from becoming a belly flop. If the puppy shifts in position left or right, use your left hand to gently, but firmly, move her back in line. Keep

doing this lesson until Daisy Dane associates the word *sit* and your firm tone with the lavish praise she will receive if she simply sits down. Soon the puppy will sit upon hearing the command alone without either the rear-end downward push or the upward pull of her head. After each successful *sit*, praise the puppy liberally and make the praise and what she had to do to get it stick out in her memory.

Again, always keep training sessions brief. To begin with, don't leave the youngster in the sitting position long enough for her to get bored with just sitting there. Gradually increase the time for sitting, always using consistent repetition and the praise reward to help Daisy Dane learn. Several brief, consistent sessions will be much more effective than one long one.

Stay

Do not attempt to teach the *stay* command until Daisy Dane has thoroughly learned the *sit* command. The *stay* is begun from the *sit*, and without that foundation, the *stay* cannot be mastered.

To begin the *stay* command, place your dog in the regular sitting position on your left. Keep some pressure on the leash in your right hand to keep your pup's head up. Giving the clear, authoritarian command, *"Stay,"* step away from the dog (moving your right foot first). At the same time, bring the palm of your left hand down in front of your Dane's face. Your command, the stepping away (always starting on the right foot), and the hand signal must be done at exactly the same time and in exactly the same way each time.

Maintain eye contact with your dog and repeat the *stay* command in the same firm tone as before. Do this several times, but don't expect long *stays* at first. Praise Daisy Dane for her *stays*, but if she moves toward you, calmly take her back to the starting point, make her *sit* and begin again with consistent repetition of the *stay* command. If the puppy seems to have trouble with *stays*, don't tire her out doing this command over and over and over again. She naturally wants to be with you, an impulse that this *stay* business stifles. At the end of each short session, if your puppy hasn't caught on to the *stay* yet, finish up with a few *sits* with a good reward for each one, thus ending the training time on a positive note. Be patient with Daisy Dane; she will learn the *stay*.

When the puppy does handle the *stay* command, praise her enthusiastically. Soon you will be able to gradually move further and further away and Daisy Dane will understand she should not move. Introduce the release word

"*okay*" in a cheerful, happy tone when you want her to stop staying and to return to you for her reward.

Heel

Once the puppy has mastered the *sit* and the *stay* commands and feels comfortable with the training collar and leash, you can begin to teach *heel*. Begin the *heel* command with Daisy Dane, in the *sit* position on your left with her head in line with your left foot. Holding the training leash in your right hand and leading off with your left foot, step forward while saying in your firm voice, "*Heel.*" As with the other commands, use the pup's name to begin the command, as in, "*Daisy Dane, heel.*"

If she doesn't move out with you when you do, smack the leash loudly against the side of your leg and repeat the command, walking away as you do. When the puppy gets the idea and catches up with you, praise her, but keep moving forward. Continue the praise and encouragement as long as she stays with you in the proper alignment.

When you stop, give the *sit* command. When Daisy Dane becomes comfortable with heeling, she will learn to sit on her own when you stop. Don't let her run ahead or lag behind or swivel around to face you. The purpose of the *heel* command is not just to walk with your dog, but to position the dog on your left and teach her to move and stop moving when you move and stop moving. The ultimate goal of teaching the *heel* command is to get your Great Dane to heel *without* use of the leash.

Never drag your puppy around just to cover some ground. If Daisy Dane has trouble with the *heel* command, go back to *sit* and start again. The *heel* may be hard for some dogs to

learn, but continue your use of consistent tugs on the leash to keep your Dane moving and to keep her head in line with your left leg. Your dog will, through consistent repetition, correction, and reward, learn to heel.

Down

Down begins with the *sit* and the *stay* commands. Using the leash in an opposite movement from the upward pull of the *sit* and *stay*, pull down on the leash with your right hand, presenting the palm of your left hand with a downward motion while giving the strong command, "*Down.*" If she is reluctant to lie down when you want her to, run the leash under your left foot and pull up on it gently, which will force her head down. Remember to repeat both the hand signal and the voice command in exactly the same way each time.

Once the puppy is in the *down* position, pour on the praise. You can help your pup in the beginning by using your left hand much in the way you do to teach the *sit*, only instead of pushing down on the hindquarters, you will push down on the back while pulling on the leash to make your dog go down on her stomach. It is the downward direction that this command emphasizes, but it should also be used with the *stay*. The ultimate goal is to cause the puppy to go straight down on her stomach on your command and to remain there until released by an *"okay"* from you.

The *down* can be a very useful and potentially important command for Daisy Dane to learn. It can be used to stop the dog in her tracks when she might be headed toward some danger. Continue to practice the *down* with the *sit* and *stay*, and be certain to thoroughly reward the dog with lavish praise when she stays put in the *down* position. By the use of patience and consistent repetition, you should be able to gradually increase the length of the *down* and even expect to leave Daisy Dane's line of sight and have her remain in place.

Come

The *come* command may seem both obvious and easy, but there are several important elements to it. Your enthusiasm and use of the dog's name while giving the command, *"Come,"* with your arms held out wide, will assure your puppy that you really want her to come to you.

Always use lots of praise on the puppy even though she is doing something she wants to do. Use the training leash and give the dog little tugs if she does come directly to you in a straight line. The *come* is another command that you will want to be obeyed immediately, not after the dog has had a chance to mark a lamppost or watch a butterfly. Treat the *come* like other commands and use your authoritarian voice and the pup's name. Danes can sometimes be a little stubborn or inattentive, but the command with the gentle (but firm) tugs on the leash should help Daisy Dane master this task. After the pup has mastered coming to you from the end of the 6-foot (1.8-m) training leash, you can switch to a longer one—up to 20 feet (6 m)—to reinforce the idea that *"Come"* means to return to you from any distance, not just a few feet away. Always reward the dog with liberal petting and praise when she comes to you.

The *come* command is somewhat different from the other basic obedience commands. It does not have to be repeated over and over again in a session. Also, you can

unexpectedly use the *come* in play sessions or just when the dog is walking in the backyard. However, you should always expect an immediate response from the dog, as she should always expect a reward of praise from you.

Never, ever make the mistake that many dog owners do and call your dog to come to you and then scold or punish her for some action! This is a form of *anti-training*. It actually teaches the dog that "sometimes when I go to the boss I get punished." This puts some doubt in her mind about whether a reward or a reprimand will be the outcome of coming to you. If a dog needs to be corrected for something, *you* go to the dog and do it; don't mess up the dog's natural impulse to want to come to you!

Obedience Training Classes

If you have never trained a dog before, you may discover that a dog training class may help you and your young Great Dane get more accomplished more effectively. Not only are these classes taught by experts who can help you help your dog learn, but this also gives you

a chance to spend some away-from-home time with your dog around other dogs and their owners in a controlled setting. If your pup shows any inclination toward aggressiveness or stubbornness, training classes—which are held several times a year in communities all over the country—may be just what you need to get your dog headed in the right behavioral direction. Ask the breeder or adoption organization where you got the puppy for any recommendations about different classes or teachers. You could find that such a class would be not only helpful, but also a lot of fun!

Note: Much of this basic training information is, of necessity, aimed at puppy training. It will also work on adult Great Danes with perhaps a little more patience and time than with inquisitive, readily moldable youngsters. Training classes are also very helpful for your adult Dane. On an additional positive note, if you have adopted an adult Dane from a foster home; your new pet will probably already be housetrained and grasp all of these basic commands!

FEEDING YOUR GREAT DANE

Great Danes require careful feeding. The requirements of this rapidly growing breed are just the start of the feeding difficulties of the Great Dane. The length of life and the quality of life will depend, to a marked degree, on what your Great Dane is fed and how he is fed.

The Importance of a Good Diet

All dogs need and deserve food that will meet their nutritional needs, that they will enjoy eating, and that can be offered in consistent and convenient ways. Diet is especially important for giant dogs like the Great Dane. Where some breeds and types of dogs can get by on average foods, Great Danes and other rapidly growing breeds simply must have a quality diet if they are to grow into their genetic potential, both physically and mentally.

The Elements of Good Canine Nutrition

There are several components or elements that make up a sound nutritional feeding program for your Great Dane. If any one of these elements is neglected or ignored, your dog's diet cannot be described as either sound or balanced. These elements are:

✔ Proteins (keeping in mind the special needs or constraints of a rapidly growing youngster)
✔ Carbohydrates
✔ Fats
✔ Vitamins and Minerals
✔ Water
✔ Owner Knowledge
✔ Owner Consistency

Proteins

Protein provides your Great Dane with the key amino acids that are so necessary for:

✔ your dog's progression through the formative stages of his life;
✔ the continued sustaining of healthy bone and muscle;
✔ the body's own repair functions on bone and muscle;

✔ the production of infection-fighting antibodies; and

✔ the production of needed hormones and enzymes that aid in natural chemical processes within the dog's body.

Carbohydrates

Carbohydrates provide fuel for your Great Dane's physical activity. Thoroughly cooked grain and vegetable products (processed starches) provide the source for most of the carbohydrates in premium-quality pet foods. Along with fats, carbohydrates are the elements in your Dane's diet that give him usable energy. Carbohydrates are measured by caloric count, or more simply, in calories.

Fats

The fats in your pet's diet provide a more concentrated energy source than do carbohydrates. In fact, the same amount of fat will provide *twice* as much usable energy as a similar amount of carbohydrates. The key vitamins—A, D, E, and K—are delivered by the fats in your Great Dane's meals. These are known as fat-soluble vitamins and are useful in helping your dog to develop and maintain healthy skin and a healthy coat.

Fats are especially important in maintaining a dog's nervous system, but they are equally significant in making dog foods more palatable. The dog foods that taste good are those more readily eaten by dogs, thus allowing a food to

be not only nutritious and balanced but also enjoyable. Lastly, fat levels are often measured against the general activity level of a dog, with the stresses of obedience work, breeding, and the show ring requiring more fats than those required for a stay-at-home "couch potato."

Vitamins and Minerals

While vitamins and minerals are certainly needed by your Great Dane for the general functioning of his body, vitamins are one of those good things that can be easily overdone. All the things a dog normally needs are supplied in a regular diet of a premium-quality dog food. Unless your veterinarian indicates otherwise, *don't* add to the vitamin and mineral levels of a good food. Additional supplementation generally does not do any good; in fact, it can actually harm your dog.

Water

Clean, fresh water is vitally important to the health of your Great Dane. Your dog will need lots of quality drinking water available to him at all times. Make pure and clean water as crucial a part of your pet's balanced diet as any of the other parts of his diet. Keep water bowls full, disinfected, and close by to maintain good health for your Dane.

Owner Knowledge

Feeding a giant dog brings with it giant responsibilities. Not only do rapidly-growing young Danes need different diets than their more average-sized counterparts, but your Great Dane's health throughout his life may largely depend on your knowledge of the food you feed him. Your Dane will be totally dependent on you for everything he regularly eats.

CHECKLIST

Balance—The Key to Good Nutrition

Because our dogs are totally dependent on us for all the food they eat, we must be absolutely certain that the diets we use are balanced. Balanced dog foods are those that scientifically contain all the necessary protein, carbohydrates, fats, vitamins, and minerals that your Great Dane will need first to grow to giant proportions, then maintain an active and healthy metabolism. There are a few major rules to follow in determining a successful feeding plan for your Dane. To avoid a poor diet and to establish a nutritionally sound feeding regimen, adhere to these basic principles:

✔ Feed your Great Dane a premium-quality, nutritionally balanced dog food.

✔ As long as a particular food is meeting your dog's needs, be consistent and stick with it. Don't constantly jump around from brand to brand.

✔ Don't overfeed, and absolutely avoid table scraps!

Your awareness of his nutritional requirements and which foods can best meet those needs will be a key part—perhaps *the* key part—of your job for your pet.

Owner Consistency

Unfortunately, for many dogs in the country their diet is composed of whatever is on sale. While most dogs can survive on the constant switching of their foods, they will simply not thrive on such a practice. This is even truer for breeds, like the Great Dane, that have been so genetically altered from the norm. While all dogs, purebred and mixed breeds alike, deserve consistent feeding of a quality food, for a Great Dane this is of even greater importance. The physical structure of a giant dog needs a lot of consistent sustenance to develop and then continue functioning.

Commercial Dog Foods

There are hundreds of pet food products available. Some are high-quality, balanced foods that may be just what you and your Great Dane are seeking. Others are inferior products that are best avoided by a dog owner in search of a nutritionally complete diet for a special pet.

One of the pluses of using a premium-quality food is that these foods normally have a toll-free number that can connect you with people experienced in canine nutrition. Don't hesitate to use these numbers to ascertain what food to feed or to ask questions about a food your Dane is already being fed.

One of the greatest truths about dog food is the old axiom, "You get what you pay for." This is certainly true about pet foods generally and about the premium-level products you will

Feeding Considerations

While opinions vary among Great Dane breeders, there seems to be some validity to the idea that feeding a young Great Dane (or any of several other fast-growing breeds) is much more difficult than feeding their more average-sized cousins. It seems that rapidly growing dogs, if fed a diet too high in protein, may put on muscle and tissue somewhat faster than their skeletal structures can grow to support the weight.

The problem that is faced in this view is that the other extreme is just as bad. If you don't feed enough protein for the muscles and tissues to develop, then the Dane can remain spindly without the true physique of the "Apollo of dogdom." Fortunately, a number of premium dog food companies now offer special foods for large-breed puppies. These companies may also have diets designed for large-breed adult dogs—like Great Danes.

Canned

Canned dog food (sometimes called wet food) is the most palatable and the most expensive way to feed your Great Dane. Canned food generally smells really good to a dog and usually is eaten with gusto, but because of its high moisture content of between 75 and 85 percent, it can also spoil quickly, even at room temperature. For a giant dog, a diet of exclusively canned food could be quite an expensive proposition. Additionally, the stool firmness resulting from eating canned food and the odor of this food is usually not as good as that of dry foods

Canned food is convenient, and its long shelf life makes it easy to keep for long periods of time. Canned food diets also tend to contribute to more dental problems than dry dog food. Most canned food is used as an additive or mixer with dry dog food for really large breeds of dogs.

want to feed your Great Dane. Don't spend a great deal of time and money finding a Great Dane, adequately housing him, providing medical care, and so forth, and then take the cheap way out when it comes to the important concept of feeding your companion. Generally, over the long term, the premium-quality dog foods are actually a much better bargain than the sale products that may seem like such a good deal.

Commercial dog foods generally come in two main forms: canned and dry. Each has some advantages and disadvantages.

Dry

Dry dog food is the most cost-effective and most popular form of dog food, especially among large dog breeders. There are a good many dry foods on the market that can be truly described as complete dog diets with real nutritional balance. Dry foods also keep well without refrigeration (which isn't true for partially used canned foods). Dry foods have somewhat of a drawback in palatability, and dogs that have only been fed canned diets may have to be taught to eat dry foods.

Because dry dog foods require more use of a pet's teeth, this form contributes somewhat to better dental health and tartar reduction on a dog's teeth. (Note: Information from some dry dog food makers notwithstanding, feeding dry food alone is not enough to keep your dog's teeth in good shape; see page 87).

Stool quality with premium-quality dry food is usually the best to be found in any form of dog diet. Digestibility is usually quite good, and puppies started on dry food readily eat it all their lives. Dry dog food does, however, have a moisture rating of only about 10 percent, making the need for good, fresh water for Great Danes all the more important.

Homemade Diets and Leftovers

Many dog breeders with years of experience may develop their own concoctions for their pets to eat, but unless you are a trained canine nutritionist or a dog breeder with lots of experience and dog food knowledge, leave homemade diets alone. Many of these are little more than nutritionally lacking meals of thinly disguised table scraps.

Table scraps have absolutely no place in a balanced canine diet. Such ill-considered snacks can keep a dog from eating the right amount of his balanced food or even, in some cases, throw the regular diet's balance completely out of whack. It is also true that feeding table scraps to your Great Dane may very well cause the big dog to expect to eat not only *what* you do, but *when* you do, and possibly *where* you do. Your dog should eat from his dish at the regular time that you set for him to eat.

Among treats that can be given safely and appropriately to your Great Dane are quality dog biscuits. Such biscuits are not only nutritionally good for your diet, but they are balanced to fit with the dog's regular diet. Follow the same rules with biscuits that you do with dog food; find a kind the dog will like and stay with them, and don't overdo it on the biscuits. Less is better than more.

Chews, like the various nylon, rubber, and rawhide items, do not necessarily fall into the category of treats. They will, however, be good for your dog. Along with providing some benefit in tartar removal (not to replace regular dental care), these items also help a teething puppy or a bored adult find a suitable alternative to the furniture to chew on.

Feeding Guidelines

Great Dane Puppies (Under Two Years Old)

There are several good foods for large breed puppies available. Using these special diets should make feeding your young Dane much simpler and better than in the past. There are two key points to remember about feeding puppies:

1. When you bring your Dane pup home, by all means get some of the *same* food he was fed at the breeder's home or foster setting. Changing diets for a puppy is tantamount to changing baby formula with a human infant. You don't do it unless you absolutely have no choice! If you continue the puppy

formats for feeding certain strains or families of Danes. An experienced Dane friend can help you find a schedule that meets both your pup's needs and your own.

Adult Great Danes (Over Two Years Old)

For some dogs, adulthood comes quickly. There are those who believe that a Great Dane will be near maturity at a little over one year old. Because of the unique problems of skeletal growth being possibly exceeded by muscular growth, feeding still-maturing youngsters according to the strict suggestions of experienced Dane people and canine nutrition experts is wise.

on the same food that he has been eating, you will reduce the transition shock that will already be in effect when your puppy leaves the only home he has ever known and moves with you to yours.

2. The second rule is similar to the first. Don't change your pup's food without an extremely good reason, and only change it with the intention of finding a puppy food that he will stay with until he reaches adulthood and goes on grown-up dog food. Responsible dog food sellers would prefer not to even give you a sample of their puppy food unless you are noticing a definite problem with what the puppy is eating now. The reason for this is both for your pup's benefit and for the benefit of the food seller. A radical, abrupt change in what a puppy is eating will almost always bring on some upset in the dog's digestive system, usually expressed in the form of diarrhea.

Young puppies will need to be fed about four times a day with a quality food. As puppies grow older, the number of feedings can be reduced to three and then finally to two as they approach adulthood. There may be other

Normally, an adult dog will receive two feedings a day. If your Dane is a prime show dog being actively campaigned at different locations each weekend, his needs will be different from the spayed or neutered Dane that lives a less active (and stressful) pet existence. The metabolism of some dogs, even littermates, may be such that some dogs will need more food than others. You can only gauge this by living with and observing the food needs of your pet.

Older Danes (Five Years Old and Older)

An older Great Dane's metabolism may begin to slow as he ages. At this point in life, the dog will need more carbohydrates and less fat in his food. There are many quality dog foods designed for older canines. These should be useful for your Great Dane, if fed moderately and consistently.

As stated, spayed and neutered Danes will usually require a diet much like older dogs, regardless of the pet's age. Remember, continued exercise is essential for spayed/neutered animals. Also remember that when feeding older pets (and spays and neuters), a fat Dane is not a healthy Dane. Added weight make the dog's internal organs have to work harder to do their jobs. A large, obese dog will also put more pressure on his feet, legs, and joints, which will contribute to laming conditions.

As with any other diet problem, such as food allergies, your best ally will be Thunder Thud's veterinarian. Long before your dog begins to have weight-related problems, discuss a possible feeding program with his doctor. You may also want to avail yourself of the experience of experienced Dane people you know to discover how they handle feeding their aging dogs.

Changing Dog Foods

While various experts disagree on the length of time you should take to make a dog food change, one good way is to do this is over a month's time. Not only does a month offer four weeks to serve as a timeline to follow, but it roughly corresponds with the amount of time some professionals believe it takes to make a new food acceptable to dogs. The key word here is *gradual*. Go from an old diet to a new diet slowly and in increasingly larger percentages over an extended period of time.

MEDICAL CARE

This giant among dogs will require very specific and highly consistent medical care throughout her life to remain in the best shape.

Special Health Needs

As in other areas of Great Dane ownership, giant dogs bring giant responsibilities with regard to medical care. Not every person can even get an immobile or unconscious dog weighing well over 100 pounds (45 kg) *into* an automobile to take her to a veterinary clinic. Giant dogs, in a way not unlike very tiny dogs, need specialized preventive and treatment measures not usually necessary for dog breeds within the broad "average" category of size. A good preventive focus to hopefully stop health problems before they occur requires a medical care "team" to deal with ongoing health issues or unavoidable conditions and a specific medical plan to help ensure Daisy Dane's well-being.

Keeping Your Great Dane Healthy

Your Great Dane deserves a safe and healthy existence. You and your family must learn accident prevention techniques and concepts. You will need to know about parasites, diseases, and other medical conditions that may arise.

Choosing Daisy Dane's veterinarian is a key decision. Most veterinary practitioners are skillful, caring professionals who offer sound care and treatment to their animal patients and solid information and guidance to their patient's owners. For your Great Dane, you will want just a little more. The health needs of giant dogs are somewhat different from the needs of many other dogs. If at all possible, try to find a veterinarian who not only has had experience with a number of the "giant" breeds (Danes, Irish Wolfhounds, Saint Bernards, Mastiffs, and so forth), but who likes big dogs as well.

Diseases and Immunizations

Not only are inoculations against an array of harmful or lethal diseases a pivotal part of your Great Dane's preventive health plan, in most places some of these illness-fighting shots are required by law!

Your Great Dane puppy should have her first immunizations at about six weeks of age while still at her first home—the breeder or foster home from where you purchased it. These initial shots were beginning vaccinations for distemper, parvovirus, canine hepatitis, leptospirosis, parainfluenza, coronavirus, and bordetella.

Preventing these diseases will necessitate follow-up shots (usually at eight to ten weeks of age and then again at twelve weeks). Another crucial immunization—for rabies—usually takes place between three and six months of age. Annual boosters may be needed for some shots.

Your puppy's shot record should be included in the permanent paperwork that you obtain when you get the puppy herself. The same thing is true if you should obtain or adopt an adult Great Dane. Your pet's veterinarian needs to know what vaccinations (or any other treatments) your dog has received before you became her owner. This complete account of what has been done to and for your Great Dane will form the foundation of your pet's health records, which should be kept current and accurate for the entire life of the dog.

Daisy Dane's veterinarian will set up a schedule for these life-saving shots. Your diligence in seeing that he is on hand to get her immunizations will be the key to the good health of your puppy. If you forget or neglect this important task, you are putting your pet at great risk.

Distemper

Distemper has a long history of tragic consequences to the world of dogs. Distemper was once the deadliest disease-enemy of puppies and young dogs. This extremely infectious and widely spread viral disease affects dogs, other canines, and some other warm-blooded animals. Raging through kennels some decades back, distemper could kill a majority of the young dogs and all of the puppies. Once struck by distemper, dogs in some kennels never recovered and went out of existence, along with the lives of most of their youngsters.

Advancements in veterinary medicine led to the development of an immunization that has greatly lowered the number of cases of this dreaded killer, but the inoculations only work if they are used. Distemper still occurs in places where dogs aren't adequately vaccinated or in wild animal populations.

A dog not immunized could begin to show symptoms as quickly as a week after coming into contact with an animal infected with distemper. Initially, distemper might seem like just a cold with a runny nose and a little fever. In most cases, the dog would "go off her feed" or simply cease eating altogether. Listlessness and an appearance of fatigue would probably be observable, with diarrhea evident in some dogs.

Distemper was once called "hard pad disease" because of the thickening rigidity of the skin on the dog's nose and foot pads. Long known to dog breeders, distemper would sometimes throw a cruel twist into its pattern of infection. Occasionally, a dog would seem to recover from the viral infection, start to regain strength, then slide back into nervous twitching, convulsions, paralysis, and finally death.

Veterinary medical science has done much to eliminate distemper from the lives of dogs and dog owners. Vaccination and yearly booster shots have made this killer of puppies and young dogs much less of a threat. Your Great Dane deserves a better fate than betting her life against distemper.

Rabies

Very few diseases evoke the level of fear that rabies, the dreaded "madness" of hydrophobia, can. Mental pictures of once-faithful dogs turning into mouth-foaming, raging monsters is still entrenched deep in the minds of people who remember when most pets were not inoculated against this acutely infectious, almost certainly fatal disease. Movies like "Ol Yeller," "Rage," and "Cujo" have reinstilled the vivid imagery of rabies into the minds of people who mistakenly been considered rabies a disease of the past.

Rabies is most often transmitted through the saliva of an infected animal, which passes the disease on by biting some other creature. Most warm-blooded mammals, including human beings, can be potential victims of rabies, but it is thought to be most often spread through skunks, bats, raccoons, foxes, unvaccinated cats and dogs, and other small animals.

In some places, rabies is still relatively widespread, with outbreaks of the disease surfacing every few years. Other areas, like the United Kingdom, have effectively eradicated rabies largely through a widespread prevention program and stern quarantine restrictions. Until 1885, when Louis Pasteur developed the first vaccine against rabies, this disease meant almost certain death. Before its fatal outcome, rabies would present certain classic signs. The first of these was the symptom that gave the disease its technical name—*hydrophobia*—meaning "fear of water." Two phases also were usually seen; the furious phase, when the animal would attack anything and everything around it. Sometimes the infected animal died in this phase, but if not, rabies progressed into the second phase—the dumb or more inactive stage, which ends in paralysis, coma, and death.

Daisy Dane is a large and generally active dog. Rabies in her would represent a significant threat to you, your family, and others. Immunization at three to six months of age, with another inoculation at one year of age followed by annual rabies shots thereafter will protect her from this horrible and now very unnecessary death.

Leptospirosis

This bacterial disease, which primarily damages the kidneys, is commonly spread through drinking or coming into contact with water contaminated by the urine of an infected animal. Symptoms of leptospirosis are loss of appetite, fever, vomiting, diarrhea, and abdominal pain.

In advanced cases, leptospirosis can quite severely damage the liver and kidneys with resultant jaundice, weakened hind quarters, mouth sores, and weight loss. Immunization for leptospirosis and annual booster shots are usually enough to protect your Great Dane.

Hepatitis

Infectious canine hepatitis can affect any member of the canine family and can be contracted by dogs at any age. The severity of hepatitis (which is not the same illness of the same name that affects humans) can range from a relatively mild sickness to a quickly fatal viral infection that can take the life of an infected dog within 24 hours from its onset.

Infectious canine hepatitis symptoms can include listlessness, fever, blood in stools, vomiting, abdominal pain, light sensitivity of the eyes, and tonsillitis. As an infectious disease,

hepatitis can be spread by contact with the feces or urine of an infected animal. Immunization with a yearly booster is a good preventive measure.

Parvovirus

This viral disease is a serious killer, especially of puppies, but it can mean death to an unvaccinated or untreated dog at any age. Parvovirus primarily attacks the gastrointestinal tract, but it can also damage the heart. Puppies with parvovirus can suffer from severe dehydration and may die within 48 hours after the onset of the disease.

While good veterinary care can save some parvovirus victims, immunization is a much better course of action. If your unimmunized puppy were to encounter a parvovirus-infected dog, your Great Dane could be infected with

a debilitating disease with potentially fatal consequences. Puppy vaccination followed by annual follow-up shots should keep parvovirus away from your pet.

Parainfluenza

Sometimes identified under the wrong name (kennel cough), parainfluenza is a highly infectious viral disease than can rapidly rage through a dog population, such as in a kennel or home where several dogs live. It is thought to be spread by contact with infected animals and the places they live, as well through the air. Parainfluenza causes a condition called tracheobronchitis, which is usually identified by a dry, hacking cough followed by retching as an attempt to cough up throat mucus. In and of itself, parainfluenza is not usually a serious illness. Untreated, however, tracheobronchitis can weaken your dog and make her vulnerable to other ailments and infections.

Parainfluenza is preventable by vaccination in the puppy series with annual reinoculation. Treatment for this disease is best supplied by a veterinarian, with the canine patient isolated from other dogs to decrease the chances of further contagion.

Coronavirus

Unvaccinated dogs of any age can be affected by this contagious disease, which can cause severe diarrhea with watery, loose, foul-smelling, bloody stools. Coronavirus is sometimes mistaken for parvovirus and may leave a dog in such a weakened condition that parvovirus or other infections may occur.

Treatment by your Great Dane's veterinarian is usually successful, but immunization by vaccine is the preferred course. By preventing this relatively mild ailment, you may be able to avoid putting your pet at risk for some of the more serious medical problems.

Bordetella

Bordetella is a bacterial infection often observed in the presence of tracheobronchitis. Bordetella may make treatment for the parainfluenza-induced tracheobronchitis more difficult. Protect Daisy Dane from this infectious "fellow traveler" by getting your pet immunized to help prevent the infection's occurrence.

Spirochetosis (Lyme Disease)

Spirochetosis (or Lyme disease) is a serious, potentially fatal disease that affects warm-blooded animals and humans. Since your Great Dane can often greatly benefit from a walk in the park or any wooded area, the possibility of

exposure to Lyme disease must be considered. This ailment could even be contracted in your pet's own backyard.

Lyme disease was first identified in Lyme, Connecticut, and is spread by the deer tick, a tiny little bloodsucker credited with carrying an illness that can do your Dane, or even *you*, great physical harm! Spirochetosis, the technical name for this disease, can affect your dog in several ways, but usually a swelling and tenderness around the joints is observable. If you find a tick on your un–Lyme-immunized dog, or suspect that the dog has been bitten by a tick, immediate veterinary care is advisable.

If *you* have been bitten by a tick or notice a tick bite with its characteristic surrounding of red (somewhat like a bull's-eye on a target), take the same action, substituting your physician or local health care for the veterinarian. In both cases, yours and the dog's timely diagnosis and treatment is essential.

If you and Daisy Dane live in an area where the deer tick is also present, take the preventive measure of immunization certainly for your dog and possibly for yourself (when a human vaccine becomes readily available). If you don't take this safety step, you and your Great Dane could be at risk every time you go out in the woods in some parts of the country.

Other Medical Conditions, Illnesses, and Concerns

Bloat/Gastric Torsion (GDV)

Bloat or gastric torsion is a very serious health concern for all of the large, deep-chested breeds of dogs, which certainly includes the Great Dane. Bloat, which has been known to painfully kill an otherwise healthy dog in just a few hours, involves a swelling of the dog's stomach from gas, water, or both. The stomach then twists, creating an internal balloon effectively sealing off the stomach from anything going in or out. Bloat still remains somewhat of a mystery but is apparently brought on by a wide variety of suggested causes that may work independently or in combination with one another. Some of these are:

- a large intake of food, followed by a large intake of water, followed by strenuous exercise;
- a genetic predisposition in some breeds, and even within some families within some breeds;
- stress, brought about by many things (one English Great Dane authority even suggested that thunder could be a contributing factor to bloat); and
- the sex and age of the dog; males seem to be affected more than females and dogs over twenty-four months of age are affected more than younger animals.

Regardless of the causes, bloat remains a real killer of large breed dogs. When a dog suffers from bloat some bloat symptoms are:

- obvious abdominal pain and noticeable abdominal swelling;
- excessive salivation and rapid breathing;
- pale and cool-to-the-touch skin in the mouth; and
- a dazed and "shocked" look.

A dog with bloat needs immediate care if she is to stand any chance of survival. Transport your Dane *immediately* to the *nearest* veterinarian, who may (and only *may*) be able to surgically save your dog's life.

Diarrhea and Vomiting

Some diarrhea and vomiting is the result of ordinary things like changes in food or some added stress. In puppies, vomiting and diarrhea can also be commonly caused by internal parasites. Even so, both diarrhea and vomiting can be early warning signals of more serious ailments.

Any extended period (more than twelve to twenty-four hours) of vomiting or diarrhea should alert you to the need for a quick trip to the veterinarian. Even if this early alarm is a false one, the next one may not be.

Anal Sac Impaction

The anal glands lie just under the skin on each side of the anus. Normally these sacs are emptied naturally when the dog defecates. When these sacs become stopped up or impacted, they must be emptied of their strong-smelling secretions by hand. One sign of impacted anal sacs is when a dog scoots along the floor dragging her rear end. The anal sacs can be emptied by your veterinarian, or you could easily learn to do this yourself.

Inherited Conditions

Almost every breed of dog will have one or more conditions that are passed along genetically from generation to generation. A tendency toward bloat or hip dysplasia could be examples of such inherited conditions. You need to be all the more certain when purchasing or adopting a young Great Dane that the dog comes from parents who have no apparent physiological deformities or other negatives that could become a negative inheritance for their offspring.

Giving Your Dane Medicine

You should know how to give Thunder Thud the medicines prescribed by his veterinarian for treatment or prevention purposes. Some dogs simply don't like to take medicine and will actually spit out pills and capsules. Some experienced dog medicine givers hide the pill or capsule in a dog treat such as bread covered with some canned dog food, or perhaps a little clump of semimoist food with the medicine hidden inside.

Other dog people take the more direct approach of opening the dog's mouth, slightly leaning his head back a short way, and then placing the pill as far back on the dog's tongue as they can reach. Once this is accomplished, they can simply close the dog's mouth, speaking calmly, and wait for the dog to swallow. (Note: *Never* tilt the Dane's head far back and simply toss in the pill or capsule; this could cause the pill to go into the windpipe instead of down the throat.)

Liquid medicine is administered in a similar way to pills and capsules. Remembering to keep the head back only a little way, simply pour the medicine into the pocket formed by the corner of the dog's mouth. Speak soothingly as you close the Dane's mouth and wait for the dog to swallow.

Always faithfully follow the veterinarian's dosages and instructions carefully. Never use outdated medicines or give your Great Dane medication designed for humans or other animals without advance approval from your dog's veterinarian.

Hip Dysplasia (HD)

Hip dysplasia is another major canine health problem. While it does not have the usually fatal consequences of gastric torsion, HD can be quite painful and debilitating. HD is a medical condition in which the hip joint is slack or loose, combined with a deformity of the socket of the hip and the femoral head joining the thigh bone. Malformed development of the hip's connecting tissues leaves an unstable hip joint. Instead of being a stable fitting (like a cup) for the end of the thigh bone, the HD-affected hip socket is usually quite shallow. HD can cause a wobbling, unsteady gait, which can be very painful to the dog.

HD is thought to be clearly inherited, but it must be acknowledged that not every puppy produced by dysplastic parents will have HD.

It is also true that some nondysplastic parents will produce some dysplastic puppies.

HD cannot always be discovered until a puppy is somewhat older. The Orthopedic Foundation for Animals (OFA) has developed a widely used X-ray method of determining the presence or absence of HD. If possible, you should get a Great Dane puppy from a mating in which both parents have been tested and found free of this condition. This should reduce the chances of your pup having this painful malady. If adopting an older Dane, discuss the possibility of the dog having HD with the foster or adoption association. For testing puppies the PennHIP test from the University of Pennsylvania can assess a pup for HD.

Wobbler Syndrome

This is an ailment that affects the neck of some Danes. There are many monikers for wobbler syndrome, which manifests itself with an unsteady "wobbling" of the hindquarters of primarily giant breeds and some large breeds. Great Danes seem to be the breed most often affected. This is a neurological disease that many authorities believe may have an inherited basis. Veterinarians have a number of diagnostic tools to help determine if a dog has wobbler syndrome. Treatment includes surgery and/or treatment with anti-inflammatory drugs.

Hypothyroidism

This condition is typically inherited and affects the immune system. Essentially, a Great Dane's thyroid doesn't produce a sufficient amount of hormone for the dog's metabolism. This ailment, characterized by skin problems and similar indicators, can be discovered with an ordinary blood test. As a chronic ailment, hypothyroidism must be treated for the remainder of the Dane's life with hormone replacement therapy.

There are other less common potentially deadly or disabling conditions that can be identified by Daisy Dane's veterinarian. Various treatment modalities, success stories, and frequency of these conditions are discussed in Great Dane circles and websites.

Internal Parasites

Dogs and puppies often have worms. Worms are parasites that draw their sustenance off your pet, and they can lead to some serious health problems. Through some simple tests, not only can your veterinarian detect the presence of worms, but he can also prescribe an appropriate treatment that will lead to their elimination. (Note: Let your veterinarian treat your Great Dane for worms. Even though various worm treatments are available on the commercial market, your dog's doctor will best know how to treat your pet for these parasites in the most effective and safest manner.)

Regular checkups will spot most parasites, but if you suspect that your Great Dane is being bothered by a parasitic infestation, don't wait until the next regular visit. The sooner your veterinarian confirms your suspicions and starts treatment, the better it is for Daisy Dane.

Worms are usually discovered by examination of your dog's stools or blood. The most common worms affecting dogs are roundworms, hookworms, tapeworms, and heartworms. Each of these parasites must be dealt with in its own specific way, which is best identified and handled by your veterinarian.

Roundworms

Even though dogs of all ages can have a roundworm infestation, puppies are the most common target of roundworms. Puppies often get roundworms even before they are born, since an infected mother dog can pass these parasites along to her offspring prenatally.

Roundworms are like weights pulling down a puppy's vitality, as pups with roundworms simply will not thrive. Roundworms take away the sharp and shiny look that a healthy puppy should have. A pendulous abdomen or potbelly may look cute on a puppy, but it is also a possible indication of roundworms. Puppies with roundworms may pass some of them through their stools or when they vomit. Recognize that roundworms sap the vim and vigor (and possibly the overall health) of your Dane puppy, who needs every edge she can get to grow up into a good and healthy representative of a giant breed. If you discover roundworms, don't delay; get your puppy into a veterinarian's care to rid her of these health-robbing interlopers.

Another thing you can do to prevent roundworm infestation is to practice good kennel hygiene. Keep Daisy Dane's living area extremely clean and sanitary. Be especially vigilant in quickly and appropriately disposing of any and all stools.

Hookworms

Another uninvited internal pest that can strike dogs of any age and really hurt puppies is the hookworm. Puppies with hookworms will have bloody or tar-like stools and will also fail to thrive. Hookworm-infested puppies don't eat properly and fail to maintain their weight.

Since hookworms are like tiny vampires that attach themselves to the insides of the small intestines and literary suck blood, they can rapidly reduce a puppy to a greatly weakened state. Anemia is sometimes a fatal consequence of leaving hookworms untreated in a puppy.

Your veterinarian knows how to handle these little bloodsuckers and how to put your puppy on the road to a healthy adulthood. As with hookworms, cleanliness is a definite part of a successful treatment plan, so get rid of stools as soon as possible.

Tapeworms

Fleas are the common host for tapeworms and can share these parasites with your dog. Though they rarely severely debilitate a dog, these flat, segmented parasites negatively affect your dog's health. A dog with tapeworms cannot be at her optimal healthy state. If you care for and want to see Daisy Dane grow into her full potential, then tapeworms are your adversary. Eliminating tapeworms from your dog will give her the added vitality to get and remain healthy.

Consult your veterinarian about a treatment plan for the elimination of tapeworms. Also ask about how to do away with the parasite that brought its parasite—the flea—to your pet. The elimination of a recurrent tapeworm infestation is just another good reason for also eliminating fleas from your dog's life.

Heartworms

Another parasite of a parasite, the heartworm comes to your pet from its original host, the mosquito. A heartworm-infested mosquito bites your dog and passes along the heartworm larvae into your pet's bloodstream and ultimately to the bloodstream's pump—the heart.

Because you will probably not want to keep your Great Dane in a mosquito-free, indoor environment every second of her life, a mosquito with heartworm larvae is ready to share its ever-present threat in most areas of the United States. The odds of your pet contracting heartworm outside are high when she is in an area where heartworms exist. Left untreated, heartworms will almost literally strangle your dog's heart and certainly cause her premature death.

Your veterinarian can help you with a plan that will prevent heartworm infestation. This involves you regularly administering medicine to kill heartworms. It must be given to a dog that does not yet have an infestation and could harm a dog who is already affected.

Treatment for heartworms is a long, potentially risky, and sometimes expensive procedure. Prevention is, by far, the better course of action and could save Daisy Dane from an early and miserable death.

External Parasites

Fleas

Fleas are the bane of a dog's existence. They are the most common external parasite afflicting dogs, and they actually feed on your Great Dane's blood. In extreme cases, fleas can bring about anemia in your dog, and in almost all cases do make a dog's life miserable. Fleas add insult to injury because not only are they an external parasite, but they harbor and introduce the internal parasite—the tapeworm—into your dog. Some dogs (like some humans) can even have an extreme allergic reaction to flea bites.

Dogs with a flea bite allergy suffer far more than nonallergic dogs. This allergy can cause hair loss, skin problems, and incessant scratching. Immediate attention by a veterinarian is required to alleviate this extremely uncomfortable condition.

Dealing with fleas involves a "take charge and take no prisoners" mentality. The sooner you realize that it is an all-out war between you and the fleas, the sooner you can begin to attack these little parasites in *every* place that they live. If Daisy Dane has fleas, everywhere that she goes will have fleas—her bed, the yard, the kennel, the car, and your home.

Failure to hit your flea enemy in any one of these battlefields (and probably several others that you can name) is as good as a complete failure. If fleas can survive in the yard, merely getting them out of the house is only a temporary victory. The fleas will be back in your house in no time.

By consulting with your veterinarian and perhaps a friend in the pet supply business, you should be able to obtain a variety of weapons in your flea war. Flea dips, flea shampoos, flea powder, flea collars, and flea spray are all remedies to use on your dog. Their use should be approved by your veterinarian and be based on the knowledge that fleas spend 90 percent of their time *off* your dog and 10 percent of their time *on* your dog.

To take care of the 90 percent of the time that fleas inhabit your yard, your car, your couch, and so forth, you must use other products. Consult with your exterminator about how to handle fleas that are not *on* your dog. Always use flea killers with great care and follow their directions implicitly!

Ticks

Ticks are another external parasite that can make a dog's life more uncomfortable. Like fleas, ticks also live on the host creature's blood. Because ticks are much larger than fleas, they suck more blood and can actually increase their size by several hundred percent—all at the expense of your dog.

While ticks are generally just a nuisance, they can carry life-threatening diseases (see Lyme Disease, page 75). They can also cause infectious sores and scars on your Dane if the ticks are removed incorrectly. Not only are these sores painful, but because of the Great Dane's short coat, they can also be somewhat unsightly.

Ticks can be prevented or eliminated fairly easily with the regular use of veterinarian-recommended sprays or dips to apply to your dog, as well as treatments for your living area. It is important to remember never to simply pull a tick off your Dane. Doing so will probably leave part of the tick's mouth in your dog's skin, which can lead to infection. To remove ticks follow these steps:

- Place a small amount of rubbing alcohol at the exact site of the tick bite. Be careful that the dog doesn't get any of this denatured alcohol into her mouth or eyes!
- After making certain that the pet will remain still, use tweezers to grab the tick as close to the dog's skin as possible, pulling *very* slowly on the tick's head and mouth.
- Be certain to get all of the tick out of your Dane's skin and then put additional alcohol or another antiseptic on the bite.
- Dispose of the tick in such a way that it will not get back on your dog or onto you!
- Sometimes you will see *two* ticks at one bite site: a large, blood-engorged one (the female) and a small, often dark brown one (the male). Be sure to get both ticks out of Daisy Dane's skin.

Ticks like to get into a Dane's large and evidently tick-inviting ears. Always check your dog carefully after any trips to the woods or a park, where ticks might be, or even after the dog has been in an untreated backyard.

Ear Mites

The prominent ears (trimmed or untrimmed) of Daisy Dane can also be targets of another bothersome pest—the ear mite. These microscopic mites live in both the ear and the ear canal. Their presence can cause a dark, dirty-looking, waxy material to adhere to the inner skin of the ears. These ear mites can cause dogs a great deal of discomfort, as evidenced by excessive ear scratching and violent head-shaking in an attempt to shake loose these itchy little parasites.

Your Dane's veterinarian is your best line of defense against this rather easily treated parasitic invader. Regularly inspect your dog's ears and then seek professional help if these mites (which are usually transferred from contact with other animals) are present.

Mange

There are two types of mange, and both are caused by another form of mite:

1. Red, or demodectic, mange especially affects physically vulnerable pets, like young puppies or oldsters, with ragged, ugly-looking hair loss accompanied by sometimes severe itching.
2. Sarcoptic mange (also known as "scabies") comes from a mite that actually burrows into the dog's outer layers of skin. Like red mange, scabies can cause a great deal of itching and hair loss. An additional negative to this kind of mange is that the highly

contagious scabies mite doesn't confine itself just to pets; they can also be transmitted to pet owners!

Both these manges make Daisy Dane not only uncomfortable and unsightly, but also unhealthy. For example, if left untreated, severe demodectic mange can become a systemic disease that could prove fatal! Seek the competent care of a veterinarian if your Great Dane seems to have mange, and do so immediately!

Other Skin Problems

Great Danes are sometimes prone to develop other skin problems. These might be fungal in nature. Flea bite allergy or another allergy of some sort might cause a skin condition. Stress or some other environmental factor could even bring on a skin problem. Even the color of your Dane may be a partial cause for these situations. Blue dogs, in other breeds as well as in Danes, sometimes have more skin problems than their fawn, black, or brindle peers.

Sometimes even what a dog eats could cause rashes or "hot spots" because some dogs definitely seem allergic to some food ingredients. Good housekeeping and regular attention to your pet's coat can help spot problems and parasites before they get a good start. Conferring with your veterinarian—not only after the fact but also ahead of time—will make skin problems less likely.

Emergency Care

Some veterinarians may make house calls, but in an emergency, this may not be a possible alternative. Always ask your veterinarian what to do in transporting a sick or injured

giant dog. Because they deal with such issues all the time, they may have options and alternatives you might not realize.

Being prepared for the things that can happen to bigger dogs over their smaller cousins is not unlike the things that can happen to toddlers instead of infants. Bigger children can get into more potential hurtful situations. The same thing is true for bigger dogs. After you have chosen a Dane-aware veterinarian, ask this professional to help you with a first aid kit to handle the basic bumps and scratches that fall within the skill level of a pet owner rather than necessitating a trip to the animal hospital.

Accidents

In even the best of dog-owner relationships, where as much preventive care and dog-proofing has taken place, accidents will happen. When they do, you must be prepared.

The first rule in dealing with an injured canine is: *Don't make things worse*. Rough handling can turn a simple fracture into a compound fracture, an injured back into paralysis, or a careless owner into an accident victim himself. As you assess the injury to your pet, try to do so with a clear head. Daisy Dane or Thunder Thud may mean the world to you, but if you really want to help your pet, you must act rationally. Some of the smart moves to make around an injured pet are:

- Speak in a calm and reassuring voice, as your hurt and frightened dog will pick up on any hysteria that your voice or demeanor could convey.

- Always approach any injured animal slowly and deliberately, even if the pet and you have been best friends for years. Speed may be important, but a dog bite can slow down the emergency aid process considerably.

- Gently but securely muzzle the dog (a Dane-sized muzzle would be a good item for the first aid kit). If a regular muzzle isn't available, use a necktie, a belt, or something similar.

- Attend to any immediate bleeding (see Bleeding, page 85) in an appropriate fashion.

- If you have sufficient muscle power available, put the dog on a makeshift stretcher (a table top, a sturdy piece of plywood, or even a strong tarp might work), securing the dog so she won't fall off.

- Call your veterinarian to alert him or her that you are on your way and will need help getting into the clinic.
- Drive *safely* to the clinic. Don't aggravate your Dane's injuries or endanger yourself by driving too fast.

(Note: The source of most of the serious injuries to pets, even huge Great Danes, comes when these canines collide with another species–the automobile. By not allowing your dog to run free and by being especially alert in situations where your dog could run out into a busy street or highway, you can probably avoid this most deadly of interactions.)

In areas where Great Danes live or near rural areas, it becomes equally important to prevent accidents by keeping the Dane at home. A large fawn Great Dane looks astonishingly like a deer, and during hunting season such a dog could be killed by a hunter in a case of mistaken identity.

Heatstroke

Your Great Dane pet can be your deceased ex-pet in a matter of only a few minutes if left inside an automobile with poor ventilation and high inside temperatures. This can happen in a short time on any sunny day, even when the weather is only moderately warm at 60°F (15°C). Even if the car windows are partially down, a dog can die from heatstroke in such an oven-hot situation. *Never* put Daisy Dane or Thunder Thud in such a senselessly dangerous and potentially fatal situation!

Heatstroke symptoms include a dazed look and rapid, shallow panting with a high fever. The dog's gums will appear bright red. Speed is now of the essence. You must act *immediately,* even before going to the *nearest* veterinarian.

Lower the dog's temperature by pouring cool water or a mixture of cool water and alcohol over the dog, even before heading to the animal clinic.

Bleeding

If your Great Dane appears to be bleeding, identify the source of the blood and apply firm but gentle pressure to the area. Continued bleeding, any significant blood loss, or a gaping wound will require veterinary attention, but treat any bleeding as a serious situation worthy of immediate action.

Poisoning

Your Great Dane is at risk in a number of ways, but never more so than in her own home and yard from accidental poisoning. Because we live in a chemically laden society, there are any number of toxic materials that Daisy Dane could accidentally ingest that could do her great harm. The most ironic part of the poisoning danger is that some of the things that we normally have around the house or even that we eat can kill a dog. Some of the most common toxic agents around the average dog's home are:

- antifreeze, which is extremely dangerous because it can leak out of the family car, perhaps even without our knowledge. It is deadly poison to pets and has a taste than many dogs love;
- chocolate, which in sufficient amounts can kill even a giant dog like your Great Dane;
- a number of outside plants, which are especially dangerous to a young Dane still in the chewing stages. Such landscaping standards like azalea, rhododendron, holly, and other yard plants can bring death to

your pet. Even wild plants, like mistletoe and poison ivy, have been known to bring out severe reactions in dogs. Check with your local county extension office for an up-to-date and area-relevant listing of potentially deadly plants that are either widely planted or that grow wild in your geographical area;

- some houseplants. Popular flowers and plants like dieffenbachia, poinsettia, and jade plants can be toxic. Before you bring a new pet into where houseplants are or bring plants into where your Dane lives, check with a florist or nursery to be certain they will be safely compatible; and

- some household cleaners. Keep all solvents, insecticides, pesticides, and cleaners away from places where Daisy Dane can go.

If Daisy Dane begins to act listless, has convulsions, or suffers from disoriented behavior she may have been poisoned. Other symptoms include diarrhea, vomiting, and a change in color of the mucous membranes. If you see these signs, hurry your pet to the veterinarian.

The Life Span of the Great Dane

Giant dogs do not have correspondingly giant life spans. Sadly, a Great Dane is often an old dog when members of toy or other smaller breeds are just entering middle age. That Daisy Dane or Thunder Thud, on average, may not live much past eight years old is a reality that you and your family must face when you decide to make a Great Dane a member of your family. Some Danes live longer than this, while others have even shorter natural lives.

Old Age

When the inquisitive youngster of all legs and ears becomes the distinguished old, gray-muzzled veteran, your treatment of your pet Dane must be different. The old Daisy Dane will sleep a little more, and play will be a little less vigorous. She will still love her family and want to be included; she just can't go as fast as before.

A whole new set of issues will be important now. Your Dane may need a dog food for senior canines. Her teeth and gums will need extra care. There may be some hearing loss and possible eye problems. Most of these can be handled by timely visits to the veterinarian and by your ongoing attention to the changing needs of your pet.

Areas Needing Your Ongoing Attention

Teeth

Daisy Dane will need good dental care all of her life. Tartar accumulation can bring on gum and tooth disease. You can lessen tartar and also greatly ensure good dental health for your dog by:

- regularly inspecting her teeth and gums, not only for tartar, but for signs of tooth decay and foreign objects (usually pieces of wood from the dog's chewing on sticks and so forth);
- cleaning your Great Dane's teeth at home;
- scheduling regular veterinary dental check-ups with occasional professional teeth cleaning to improve upon your efforts;
- using veterinarian-approved chew toys and dental exercisers, designed to help remove tartar and plaque; and
- feeding a good brand of dry dog food and dog biscuits that will use the dog's regular chewing and grinding action to help reduce tartar.

Eyes

The large, prominent eyes of the Great Dane will need some attention from you as the dog ages. Other than the puppy-proofing and Dane-proofing that should be a well understood part of your regular regimen, you need to protect your dog from sharp objects that might be just at eye level. You also need to keep the Dane safe from toxic substances or fumes that can irritate or damage eyes.

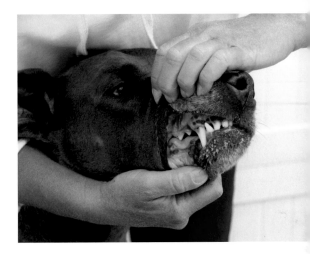

Neighborhood children throwing stones or shooting an air rifle at what is probably the biggest dog in the neighborhood could do your Dane damage. Air pollution, thorny plants, and heavy underbrush all have eye-damaging potential. Even aging itself could bring on problems like cataracts. All of these eye problems can be greatly lessened in severity by

regular eye inspections done by you and by your veterinarian during general checkups.

You may notice some mucous collecting in the corners of your Great Dane's eyes from time to time. This is usually a perfectly normal condition that can be simply dealt with by gently wiping the area with a soft cloth. Don't, however, confuse this ordinary mucous-like material with an eye discharge, which can signal an eye problem and needs professional attention.

Ears

The ears of a Great Dane are among its most striking features. Whether your Dane has had his ears cropped like many show dogs or whether your dog has his ears in the natural state, these ears will need regular attention and ongoing care from you. Dog ears are among the favorite hiding places of parasites such as ticks and ear mites (see Ticks, page 81 and Ear Mites, page 82). Regular inspection of the ears will let you spot these little invaders early and begin a plan to get rid of them.

Sometimes a male dog's ears will be a record of the hostile interactions he may have had with other male dogs. Also because of their location (high up on either side of the dog's head), ears will take some damage when a big, fast dog runs through underbrush. Always keep a close watch on your pet's ears for cuts or scratches that may need medical attention from you or a veterinarian.

Feet and Nails

Giant dogs bring giant feet and toenail responsibilities. While the feet of every dog will be better if the dog's owner gives them regular care, the feet of a huge dog who must often support a weight of more than 150 pounds (68 kg) *must* have good owner care. One owner of a large brindle male that weighed 187 pounds (85 kg) asserted, "If you don't think that the feet of a Great Dane take a lot of punishment, let my dog step on your foot with just one of his."

While a small dog might be able to get around on a bad foot or on a foot with an injured toenail, giant dogs have considerably more trouble when their running gear is injured. Beginning with good nail care (which should start when the Great Dane is a puppy) down to preventive maintenance, which keeps broken glass and other foot-harming items out of the dog's path, the care of a Dane's feet is as important as any other part of the dog's health plan.

Great Danes will put a lot of stress on their footpads and on their nails. Regular inspections will let you know if your dog has suffered a slight abrasion, which could become a bigger foot problem later. Regular nail trimming, which isn't difficult when the dog has had it done all his life, is a must for good foot care. You will need a Dane-worthy set of toenail clippers (either the scissors type or the "guillotine" type), and whichever you purchased should be used regularly as the dog's nail start to grow too long. Remember in nail trimming to keep well away from the quick of the main blood supply of the nail. You may have to use an emery board or nail file to shorten nails when the quick is too close for easy trimming.

Another aspect of foot care is to carefully look at your Dane's feet after a walk on a street, or at a paved highway rest area. Sometimes toxic substances, motor oil, or antifreeze can be picked up on a dog's feet. If the dog licks the offending substance off, feet problems can become possible poisoning.

When the End Approaches

That gangling puppy you chose will grow to become the majestic Great Dane and a full member of your family. Barring premature death from illness or accident, this majestic friend will grow to be an old Dane. In the best of all practical worlds, every good, old dog would live a full, healthy life and die painlessly in his sleep one night. In the real world things don't always work out like we would hope.

Great Danes have been given much through-out their lives. Their beauty and regal strength is admired the world over. When the Dane grows old, his size tends to work against him.

That great height and weight can become a burden for an old dog. For some Danes, the ravages of old age bring pain and discomfort to their last years.

Hopefully Thunder Thud will live out the best possible ending and never know a painful day in his life. If this does not occur and your old friend begins to suffer, a difficult choice has to be made. When living becomes unbearable for Thunder Thud, take your veterinarian's counsel and give serious consideration to painlessly ending his suffering. Such a decision is never easy, but for the good of the dog a gentle, painless, humane end is far better than endless and acute discomfort.

Prevention of any medical problem is always better than an after-the-fact treatment approach. Because Great Danes are huge dogs, they can have huge problems. Preventing health problems for such a giant breed deals with several diverse aspects of Great Dane ownership.

1. Choose a Great Dane from a physically and temperamentally sound stock. This is an essential element in an effort to avoid some painful, expensive, and heartrending circumstances later. While no dog can be absolutely guaranteed to never develop serious medical problems throughout all of his life, choosing or adopting a puppy or an adult Great Dane with a poor medical temperament heritage can greatly increase problems in the future.

2. Make sure to to prepare for a rapidly developing canine of a giant breed. Failure to do so increases the possibility that accidents will happen, and from these accidents dire consequences can result. For example, that your Dane will always be a model canine citizen and never get into trouble when running free in a neighborhood is poor thinking. If you don't have your dog under some form of control or restraint at *all* times when your Dane is outside, (a Dane-appropriate fence, a leash combined with good training) possibly fatal medical problems are *certain* to come your Dane's way.

3. Obtain regular medical care by a Dane-friendly veterinarian. This will not only eliminate many negative medical conditions, but will also spot other

situations. Treatment plans can handle these potential problems. No dog should go without immunizations and consistent veterinary medical care.

4. Because of the demand placed on the metabolism, bones, and muscle tissue of a rapidly growing Great Dane, it is important to become well-versed in canine nutrition generally, and in Dane nutrition specifically. Failure to do so can, at the very least, produce an adult that doesn't quite meet the definition of a proper Great Dane physically, mentally, or temperament-wise.

5. It is essential to train your Great Dane, at least in the basic commands for human control. A giant dog that doesn't obey is a giant problem with potentially giant consequences.

6. Hoping for the best while preparing for the worst is a sound philosophy for a new Dane owner. Even with the best care, feeding, medical attention, training, and safety-oriented environment, a puppy or an adult dog can sometimes become injured or sick. While having a good working relationship with a Dane-aware veterinarian is part of an emergency plan, there are other factors that must be considered:
   - Unless you are as large a human as your Dane is a dog, you will need to have an action plan on how to get a sick or injured pet to the animal clinic.
   - Knowledge of possible Dane-threatening conditions such as gastric torsion (or bloat) is a mandatory precondition before becoming the owner of a Great Dane and must be part of any emergency prevention plan.

- Making a home as Dane-friendly and accident-proof as possible is sometimes overlooked by potential (or existing) Dane owners. A larger-than-large dog with potential to put his forepaws higher than some humans can reach, and with a sizeable weight to back him up, can easily get into some potentially harmful predicaments. Use common sense in your home and other environments to avoid just such problems.

INFORMATION

International Kennel Clubs

Great Dane Club of America*
Marie A. Fint
442 Country View Lane
Garland, Texas 75043
www.gdca.org

*This address may change with the election of new club officers. The current listing can be obtained by contacting the American Kennel Club.

American Kennel Club
51 Madison Avenue
New York, New York 10038
www.akc.org

Australian National Kennel Council
Royal Showgrounds
Ascot Vale 3032
Victoria, Australia
www.ankc.org.au

Canadian Kennel Club
200 Ronson Drive, Suite 400
Etobioke, Ontario M9W 5Z9
www.ckc.ca

The Kennel Club
1-5 Clargis Street
Piccadilly, London, W1J 8AB
England
www.thekennelclub.org.uk

New Zealand Kennel Club
P.O. Box 523
Wellington, 1
New Zealand
www.nzkc.org.nz

Information and Printed Material

American Boarding Kennel Association
4575 Galley Road, Suite 400A
Colorado Springs, Colorado 80915
(publishes lists of approved boarding kennels)

American Society for the Prevention of Cruelty
  to Animals (ASPCA)
424 East 92nd Street
New York, New York 10128
www.aspca.org

American Veterinary Medical Association
1931 North Meacham Road, Suite 100
Schaumberg, Illinois 60173
www.avma.org

Gaines TWT
P.O. Box 8172
Kankakee, Illinois 60901
(publishes *Touring with Towser*, a directory of hotels and motels that accommodate guests with dogs)

Humane Society of the United States
2100 L Street, NW
Washington, DC 20037
www.humanesociety.org

Books

In addition to the most recent edition of the official publication of the American Kennel Club, The Complete Dog Book (published by Howell House, Inc.), other suggestions include:

Alderton, David. *The Dog Decoder.* Hauppauge, New York: Barron's Educational Series, Inc., 2011.

Arden, Andrea. *Barron's Dog Training Bible.* Hauppauge, New York: Barron's Educational Series, Inc., 2011.

Arrowsmith, Claire. *Instant Dog Training.* Hauppauge, New York: Barron's Educational Series, Inc., 2011.

Baer, Ted. *Communicating with Your Dog, 2nd Edition.* Hauppauge, New York: Barron's Educational Series, Inc., 1999.

Baxter, Roberta, and Pinney, Chris. *Mini Encyclopedia of Dog Health.* Hauppauge, New York: Barron's Educational Series, Inc., 2011.

Miller, Scott. *Puppy Parenting.* Hauppauge, New York: Barron's Educational Series, Inc., 2008.

Schlegl-Kofler, Katharina. *The Complete Guide to Dog Training.* Hauppauge, New York: Barron's Educational Series, Inc., 2008.

Tennant, Colin. *Breaking Bad Habits in Dogs, 2nd Edition.* Hauppauge, New York: Barron's Educational Series, Inc., 2010.

Wrede, Barbara. *Civilizing Your Puppy.* Hauppauge, New York: Barron's Educational Series, Inc., 1992.

I N D E X

About the Author

Joe Stahlkuppe is a widely read pet columnist, author, and freelance writer. He is a retired clergyman and lives with his wife, Cathie near Birmingham, Alabama.

Acknowledgments

As has always been the case in the numerous books I have written for Barron's, I must show deepest appreciation to my wife Cathie, son Shawn, and our grandchildren; Catie, Peter, Julia, and Alexandra.

Books don't just happen because some dog person scribbles words on a page. Barron's is blessed with a number of outstanding editors. I have been blessed with a superstar editor in Angela Tartaro. Not only is she a wonderful editor, she is also a wonderful person whose help, patience, and encouragement are true treasures!

Others should be acknowledged for many kind contributions: Ann and Jim English, Alberto "Butch" and Diane Zaragoza, Joel and Rhonda Nichols, Rocky and Dee Hicks, Kenneth and Suzzane Barnes, Dwayne and Kay Barnett, Joe and Martha Ann Still, Alan and Connie Whitworth, Linda Collier, and Linda Brown. I also want to thank my brothers and sisters for their abiding love for pets and me (probably in that order): Mary Helen, Gene (with wife Patsy), Susan, and Charlie.

Lastly, many accolades should go to the Great Danes and their loving owners who are truly GREAT, each and every one!

Cover Credits

Cheryl Ertelt: inside front cover; Shutterstock: front cover, back cover, inside back cover.

Photo Credits

123rf: pages 19, 36, 68; Kent Akselsen: pages 4, 9, 21, 29, 39; Seth Casteel: pages 27, 33, 34, 49, 50; Dreamstime: pages 18, 30, 37, 43, 48, 81, 89; iStockphoto: pages 7, 10, 11, 14, 16, 20, 46, 63, 66, 67, 71, 74, 83, 84; Daniel Johnson: pages 17, 22 (bottom), 23, 62, 87 (top), 87 (bottom); Modern Life Photo: pages 40, 60, 69; Oh My Dog! Photography: pages 26, 45, 55 (bottom); Shutterstock: pages 2, 5, 6, 8, 12, 13, 15, 23, 24, 25, 26, 28, 31, 32, 35, 41, 44, 53, 54, 58, 59, 61, 65, 66, 68, 70, 77, 86, 90; Kira Stackhouse: pages 38, 52, 55 (top); Connie Summers: pages 78, 93; Joan Hustace Walker: pages 22 (top), 56, 57, 91.

All inquiries should be addressed to:
Barron's Educational Series, Inc.
250 Wireless Boulevard
Hauppauge, NY 11788
www.barronseduc.com

Library of Congress Catalog Card No. 2012010772

ISBN: 978-0-7641-4746-3

Library of Congress Cataloging-in-Publication Data
Stahlkuppe, Joe.
    Great Danes : everything about purchase, care, nutrition, behavior, and training / Joe Stahlkuppe.
        p. cm.
    Includes bibliographical references and index.
    ISBN 978-0-7641-4746-3 (alk. paper)
    1. Great Dane. I. Title.
    SF429.G7S73 2012
    636.73—dc23   2012010772

Printed in China
9 8 7 6 5 4 3 2 1